ASHE Higher Education Report: Volume 38, Number 4
Kelly Ward, Lisa E. Wolf-Wendel, Series Editors

Study Abroad in a New Global Century: Renewing the Promise, Refining the Purpose

Susan B. Twombly

Mark H. Salisbury

Shannon D. Tumanut

Paul Klute

Study Abroad in a New Global Century: Renewing the Promise, Refining the Purpose
Susan B. Twombly, Mark H. Salisbury, Shannon D. Tumanut, Paul Klute
ASHE Higher Education Report: Volume 38, Number 4
Kelly Ward, Lisa E. Wolf-Wendel, Series Editors

Cover image by a_Taiga/©iStockphoto.

ISSN 1551-6970   electronic ISSN 1554-6306   ISBN 978-1-1185-1137-4

The ASHE Higher Education Report is part of the Jossey-Bass Higher and Adult Education Series and is published six times a year by Wiley Subscription Services, Inc., A Wiley Company, at Jossey-Bass, One Montgomery Street, Suite 1200, San Francisco, California 94104-4594.

Individual subscription rate (in USD): $174 per year US/Can/Mex, $210 rest of world; institutional subscription rate: $307 US, $367 Can/Mex, $418 rest of world. Single copy rate: $29. Electronic only–all regions: $174 individual, $307 institutional; Print & Electronic–US: $192 individual, $353 institutional; Print & Electronic–Canada/Mexico: $192 individual, $413 institutional; Print & Electronic–Rest of World: $228 individual, $464 institutional.

CALL FOR PROPOSALS: Prospective authors are strongly encouraged to contact Kelly Ward (kaward@wsu.edu) or Lisa Wolf-Wendel (lwolf@ku.edu). See "About the ASHE Higher Education Report Series" in the back of this volume.

Visit the Jossey-Bass Web site at **www.josseybass.com.**

The ASHE Higher Education Report is indexed in CIJE: Current Index to Journals in Education (ERIC), Education Index/Abstracts (H.W. Wilson), ERIC Database (Education Resources Information Center), Higher Education Abstracts (Claremont Graduate University), IBR & IBZ: International Bibliographies of Periodical Literature (K.G. Saur), and Resources in Education (ERIC).

Advisory Board

The ASHE Higher Education Report Series is sponsored by the Association for the Study of Higher Education (ASHE), which provides an editorial advisory board of ASHE members.

Contents

Executive Summary

In the context of an increasingly global society, study abroad has taken on an especially important role for colleges and universities. The education, government, and business communities are united in the call for college graduates to be competent to function in a global economy. Although a very small number of American college students have traveled abroad for educational purposes, study abroad has taken on added importance in the twenty-first century as the main way to accomplish this goal through its potential to develop a variety of intercultural competencies. Parents and students expect study abroad options, and institutions gladly offer them. Although the ambitious goal of the Commission on the Abraham Lincoln Study Abroad Fellowship Program, a congressionally established commission, to send one million students abroad annually is far from being met, the number of students studying abroad has increased steadily, reaching a high of nearly 271,000 in 2010–2011.

The push for study abroad is premised on the notion that study abroad is uniquely positioned to develop the kinds of intercultural skills needed to compete in a global economy. The expectations are high for both participation rates and outcomes. Despite the overwhelmingly positive view Americans have of the potential of study abroad, there are nagging concerns: the study abroad population remains relatively homogeneous and outcomes may have more to do with who participates than program activities. There are also critics who suggest that study abroad providers are merely promoting a twenty-first-century form of American imperialism and who even question what study abroad means in an increasingly homogeneous, flat world.

In light of these intersecting forces that position study abroad as a crucial educational tool, albeit one that is not easily available to all students, this monograph sets out to review the increasingly vast literature on study abroad. Two fundamental questions are at the center of our review: (1) who studies abroad (or who does not) and why? and (2) what are the outcomes of studying abroad? Stated differently, we seek to determine whether the outcomes of study abroad are sufficiently positive to warrant the significant investment it would take to reach the Lincoln Commission's ambitious participation goal. Our review is framed by the notion that study abroad outcomes are influenced by participant characteristics, program characteristics, and student experiences in the host culture. In order to contextualize the research addressing our two central questions, we place study abroad in historical context as well as consider critiques of it. Importantly, we include a critique of the research methods used to study the impact of study abroad.

History and Purposes

The U.S. approach to study abroad emerged between the two world wars as an extension of the European Grand Tour especially adapted for women. In its early years, the Junior Year Abroad and faculty-led study tours were the dominant form of study abroad. Over the course of the twentieth century and especially following World War II, aided by a national organizational infrastructure such as the Institute of International Education, study abroad began to expand in all ways: the number of institutions providing study abroad, the types of programs, and the number of students participating. This expansion has been aided in the post-9/11 era by national attention to the importance of study abroad in the form of blue ribbon reports and initiatives on the part of the federal government and organizations such as the American Council on Colleges and Universities and the Forum on Education Abroad. Throughout its history, the purposes of study abroad and types of programs have adapted to national objectives and to a variety of forces affecting higher education generally and institutions specifically.

Types of Programs and Providers

Identifying types of study abroad programs, once a simple task, has become a complicated affair. Most organizations categorize study abroad programs by a primary single defining characteristic, such as length, location, or who directs the program. These simple descriptors may no longer accurately capture the complexity of an individual program or its outcomes. As a result, new schemes have been proposed that allow providers and researchers to map program characteristics onto levels of immersion or some other way of differentiating program expectations. The resulting mapping has the potential to better capture the complex expectations of study abroad and to differentiate outcomes between, for example, a junior abroad immersion experience and a short-term study abroad experience. Providers of study abroad programs continue to include higher education institutions as well as third-party providers.

Who Studies Abroad and Who Does Not

Despite all of the attention study abroad has received, it remains an activity in which a tiny percentage of U.S. undergraduate students participate. Moreover, although there have been some slight changes in percentages of men, students of color, and STEM (science, technology, engineering, and mathematics) majors participating in study abroad, study abroad participation remains the domain of women, white students, and humanities and social science majors. The one notable departure from this pattern is an increase in participation among business majors. Reasons for these participation patterns are complex and vary by gender and race/ethnicity and major. Cost, or perceived cost, is a universal and expected obstacle. A more surprising deterrent for male students involves peer interactions.

Outcomes

Numerous studies link study abroad participation to a wide range of positive outcomes, including intercultural competence, global perspectives, personal growth and identity, academic interest, graduate degrees, and career success. Recent studies also show that study abroad participation does not deter graduation or delay graduating on time and may actually improve rates of both. Research on study abroad outcomes must be understood in light of methodological weaknesses, such as small, single institution studies and inability to control for all of the variables one needs to control for in order to isolate the unique contribution of study abroad apart from individual student characteristics, and to understand how the different types of study abroad experiences affect outcomes.

Critical Perspectives

Counteracting the positive vision of study abroad, critics raise important questions about the purpose, the homogeneity of study abroad participants, and the experience of study abroad. Those who question the purpose of study abroad challenge its role as an instrument of American imperialism and commercialism, suggesting that the objective of creating "global citizens" is an imperialistic act of the United States. Others challenge the very meaning of study abroad in a globalized world. Qualitative researchers who have studied the experience raise important questions about the experience itself and provide implications for understanding the outcomes of study abroad.

Conclusions, Final Thoughts, and Recommendations

Policymakers and educators have high hopes and expectations for study abroad. And, while much of the research suggests positive outcomes, this review suggests that the outcomes may not be as overwhelmingly positive as educators wish to believe or as warranted by the substantial investment of time and resources required by institutions and individuals. In order to meet the educational challenges of the twenty-first century, study abroad must shift from a focus on perpetually increased participation to purposefully designed educational impact. This can be done by explicitly designing and delivering each study abroad program around clearly identified educational outcomes; by not assuming that any and all study abroad experiences improve intercultural competence; by aligning study abroad outcomes with an appropriate developmental model of learning; by reconceptualizing study abroad as part of an integrated educational experience; by reframing how institutions assess the impact of study abroad; by asking whether study abroad, as currently defined, is the best means of accomplishing specific learning outcomes; and finally, by changing the metric by which study abroad participation is judged from how many to which students.

Foreword

There are few formal college activities that are seen by almost everyone—including the broader public—as being uniformly positive. Study abroad is one such activity. Positive outcomes seemingly abound from participating in study abroad—it improves retention, it improves academic performance, it helps students learn language and culture, it deepens students' openness to diversity, it broadens students' horizons, it helps them develop into adulthood, it even might be a key to attaining world peace. Study abroad is included by many on the short list of activities that all but ensure college success (along with service learning, learning communities, internships, and undergraduate research). Indeed, I can think of few other college activities that are so uniformly positively regarded as is study abroad. The audience who thinks positively about study abroad is also vast—the U.S. government, foreign governments, businesses, students, faculty, administrators, and even the general public tout the positive outcomes of study abroad. But, questions remain unanswered about study abroad. It is the ultimate black box—a student participates and somehow positive outcomes are accrued. How does this happen? What is it about study abroad that leads to such outcomes? How much time does one need to spend abroad to benefit? Does it take a week, a month, a full term, or a full academic year? Does spending more time lead to more benefits? Are there certain aspects of a study abroad program that lead to more positive outcomes—for instance, is it better to live in a residence hall or with a family, to immerse oneself in the culture, or hang out with other American students? Is coursework necessary—if yes, what kind? Is it better to take courses at the university in the foreign country or can a class taught with U.S.

faculty on foreign soil suffice? Based on the research conducted to date, it appears that we do not really know the answers to these questions. The present monograph, however, does help to lay out answers to some of these questions and to highlight what we still don't yet know about this popular college program.

Susan Twombly, Mark Salisbury, Shannon Tumanut, and Paul Klute, in this monograph on study abroad titled "Study Abroad in a New Global Century: Renewing the Promise, Refining the Purpose," have brought a much needed critical lens to this important topic. As noted by the authors, methodological problems abound with researching study abroad. It is difficult to determine who one should compare participants with—what kind of appropriate control group is there when it comes to study abroad? Further, since every study abroad program has different components, it is difficult to find studies that look at more than one program at a time. Among the helpful components of this monograph include a mapping of types of study abroad and a discussion of who provides and organizes the activities. The monograph also explores who does and does not study abroad. As noted by the authors, study abroad programs and their positive outcomes are largely influenced by the high quality though homogenous nature of students who participate—trying to make study abroad more accessible to a wider array of students has thus far been relatively ineffective due to issues such as cost, time, and other resources. Further, although the authors clearly are positive about study abroad and its benefits, they are among the first to offer a critical perspective of these programs. These critical perspectives are largely absent from the mainstream literature that looks at study abroad in a higher education context.

This monograph, like others in the series, is written for a host of audiences. It will be of interest to those who work in study abroad programs, those who fund such programs on college campuses, as well as to those who study their outcomes. It will be useful to both scholars and practitioners. It is written to appeal to a broad audience—simplifying the landscape of research on study abroad and complicating it at the same time. While there are no other ASHE Higher Education Reports on this same topic, there are some that might be of relevant interest to those who read this monograph. These include the recent monograph on *Engaged Diversity in the Classroom* by Amy Lee and her colleagues, *Reinventing Undergraduate Education* by Shouping Hu and colleagues, and *Piecing Together the Study Success Puzzle* by George Kuh and his colleagues.

Lisa E. Wolf-Wendel
Series Editor

Published online in Wiley Online Library
(wileyonlinelibrary.com) • DOI: 10.1002/aehe.20004

Introduction

D URING THE PAST DECADE the entire U.S. higher education enterprise, from community colleges to umbrella associations such as the American Association of Colleges and Universities, as well as the federal government and the business community, have promoted and encouraged study abroad as a means for colleges and universities to graduate students who are interculturally competent. Such competence is vital, these stakeholders argue, for all manner of future success—be it personal or professional, individual or societal. The literature of a wide range of higher education institutions, as well as those of higher education associations such as the American Council on Education (ACE), is replete with terms such as *global society, international awareness,* and *interconnected world* (Lewin, 2009). Colleges and universities have responded by internationalizing their programs. One has only to peruse institutional websites to conclude that regardless of institutional size or mission, the international dimension is front and center.

Although this commitment to academic internationalization varies from college to college, study abroad consistently appears as a primary means of developing global and intercultural competence among American students. By 2006 over 90 percent of all colleges and universities offered study abroad (Hoffa and DePaul, 2010). Moreover, each college offers many programs of different types and in many different countries. The University of Kansas claims, "Over 100 programs of international study and cooperative research are available for KU students and faculty at sites throughout the world" (University of Kansas, n.d.). Mount Holyoke encourages "language immersion, field studies,

---

or traditional classroom based programs in more than 50 countries" (Mount Holyoke College, n.d.).

A segment of American undergraduate college students has always spent some portion of their college years studying in a foreign country to learn languages and gain cultural refinement, to experience adventure and learn about oneself, and to develop intercultural competence (Bowman, 1987; Hoffa, 2007). Graduate students have gone abroad to acquire professional education or in the nineteenth century to earn a PhD (Lucas, 2006). Aspects of each of these individual motivations for studying abroad have remained constant even as the rationales for study abroad have shifted in concert with the changing landscape of American higher education and international dynamics. At various times the rationales have emphasized study abroad as a means to promote peace through understanding or to promote democracy and counteract Communism. Today the rationale for colleges to encourage study abroad and for students to take part is frequently cast in economic terms. In the "flat world" Thomas Friedman describes, individuals must be globally competent not to prevent war but to compete economically (Friedman, 2005). Such competence is portrayed as essential, not an option (Fischer, 2007). From the institutional point of view, reasons for offering study abroad have also shifted over time from providing students with a sort of culturally elite "finishing school" to demonstrating to an increasingly savvy public the degree to which an institution is proactively preparing its students for a globally interconnected future (Bolen, 2001).

Calls for increasing global awareness and global competency through study abroad have come from far and wide: former president Clinton, scholars such as Martha Nussbaum and former Harvard president Derek Bok, and nearly every higher education association. In the past decade, the American Association of Colleges and Universities (AAC&U), Association of Public and Land-Grant Universities (APLU), and the American Council on Education (ACE) have all engaged in major projects to promote an increase in global awareness, including study abroad options. The federal government, long a promoter of international exchange including study abroad, also sees renewed value in having a globally competent citizenry to ensure that the United States remains a vital and stable society. In its final report, the Commission on the Abraham Lincoln Study Abroad Fellowship Program (2005), a congressionally appointed commission, argued that there is a national need to "[c]reate a more globally informed American citizenry; increase participation in quality study abroad programs; encourage diversity in student participation in study abroad; diversify locations of study abroad, particularly in developing countries; create an innovative partnership with higher education to open more doors for study abroad, and internationalize U.S. higher education by making study abroad a cornerstone of undergraduate education" (NAFSA, 2009a).

Accordingly, the Senator Paul Simon Study Abroad Act was introduced to Congress. The Act proposed making available considerable resources for students to study abroad, specifically students from community colleges and minority-serving institutions (NAFSA, 2009b). The Lincoln Commission and Senator Paul Act (H.R. 1469/S. 991, 2007; S. 473, 2009), although not funded, both provided important rhetorical statements about the critical importance of the study abroad experience, albeit one best paid for by the students themselves rather than the federal government. Perhaps most important, they set new and ambitious goals for the number of students that should study abroad.

Colleges and universities as well as students and their parents seem to have responded to the message advocating the importance of study abroad. The number of U.S. students participating continues to increase at a steady clip regardless of fluctuations in the economy, reaching a record 270,604 students in 2009–2010 (Institute of International Education [IIE], 2011). This represents a 44 percent increase since 2000–2001 and a 72 percent increase since 1989–1990 (IIE, 2011). In addition, the number of institutions offering study abroad has increased. By 2006 over 90 percent of all colleges and universities offered study abroad (Hoffa and DePaul, 2010). In recent years even U.S. community colleges have begun study abroad programs (Hoffa, 2007). Since 2003/2004, community colleges have been sending students abroad at the rate of about 6,000 students per year (IIE, n.d.e). Not surprisingly, the array of available programs has also increased substantially as students seek out more exotic locations in which to study. In 1998–1999, the majority of students studied in Europe—England in particular. Although European countries still remain some of the most popular study abroad destinations, the countries seeing the greatest increases as destination sights in 2009–2010 were India and Israel (IIE, 2011).

Moreover, as study abroad has come to occupy a more central role in undergraduate education in the twenty-first century, institutions have increasingly highlighted their efforts to promote study abroad, touting the percentage of students studying abroad as an important indicator of institutional global engagement. IIE now provides rankings of the "top colleges" for study abroad (IIE, n.d.a). This, in turn, has surely contributed to the broader perception—if not outright reality—that study abroad has emerged as a core academic offering with substantial benefits for the individuals who participate, the institutions that successfully foster that participation, and the global economic positioning of the United States.

A reading of the research literature suggests that the investment in study abroad is a good one. Research suggests that study abroad has significant beneficial outcomes for students. Students who have studied abroad become more globally aware (in addition to many other positive outcomes) after a study abroad experience (Clarke, Flaherty, Wright, and McMillen, 2009; Dessoff, 2006; Dolby, 2004, 2007; Fuller, 2007; Hadis, 2005; Jessup-Anger, 2008; Kitsantas and Meyers, 2001; Kitsantas, 2004; Olson and Kroeger, 2001; Younes and Asay, 2003). In most cases, studying abroad has a positive impact on academic performance post-sojourn as students become more interested in academics (Malmgren and Galvin, 2008). However, there is a literature that raises questions about the commercialization of study abroad and its effects on the purposes and outcomes of study abroad programs (Bolen, 2001; Engle and Engle, 2002; Zemach-Bersin, 2007), the outcomes of study abroad (Citron, 2002; Salisbury, 2011; Talburt and Stewart, 1999; Twombly, 1995; Wilkinson, 1998a, 1998b, 2000), and the very meaning of study abroad in a post-nation state, more globalized and interconnected world (Engle and Engle, 2002; Hoffa, 2002). Certainly, while the number of study abroad participants has increased, the goals of the Lincoln Commission and the Paul Simon Act are far from reach.

Monograph Purpose

In light of these intersecting forces positioning study abroad as a crucial educational tool for achieving ambitious outcomes, this review seeks to answer two central questions: (1) who studies abroad (or who does not) and why? and (2) what are the outcomes of studying abroad? Stated somewhat differently, are the outcomes of study abroad sufficiently positive to warrant the significant investment it would take to reach the Lincoln Commission's ambitious participation goal? That is, does the research provide information that will help to improve participation, and does participation lead to the globally competent citizens that the Lincoln Commission's recommendations assume?

Participation in study abroad and outcomes of study abroad must be considered in context. Consequently, who participates and the expected outcomes are framed by the reality that, in addition to being influenced by participant characteristics, study abroad outcomes are influenced in no small way by program characteristics and student experiences in the host culture. Participation and program types and characteristics are in turn shaped by the history and purposes of study abroad. To this end, the monograph also addresses the question of how the history of study abroad has shaped the purposes of study abroad and program types. Because the literature on study abroad is so overwhelmingly positive in its tone, sometimes in the face of modest results, we also look to the critiques of study abroad research as well as to the critiques of purpose and experience to examine how insights from these voices might inform the promise of preparing globally competent citizens.

The concluding chapter of this monograph addresses three questions based on findings from the review:

1. Does study abroad meet the lofty goals of preparing interculturally competent citizens?
2. Can it reasonably be expected to do so?
3. How might study abroad be organized differently to achieve these goals?

Conceptual Framework

A conceptual framework composed of three main ideas guides our review:

1. Stephenson's "thematic triad: sojourner,[1] host culture and program" (2002, p. 89) provides a framework for thinking about the factors that impact study abroad outcomes.

2. Rodman and Merrill's (2010) conceptualization of study abroad design resulting from three levels of influence on study abroad programs—the macro (societal), mezzo (higher education), and micro (institutional/program)—focuses on factors that influence program design.
3. Paulsen and St. John's (2002) student choice construct helps us understand who plans to study abroad.

In attempting to understand and explain why some study abroad students achieve "cross-cultural deepening" while others do not, Stephenson (2002) identifies three sets of factors "that serve to influence the process and outcome of the cross-cultural experience for study abroad students" (p. 90). The areas or sets of factors are: individual characteristics, characteristics of and opportunities to interact with the host culture, and characteristics of the study abroad program and its staff (pp. 90–93). Within each area, Stephenson posits a series of characteristics along continuums of having more or less impact on cross-cultural deepening. For example, among individual factors, she lists "less language skill vs. more language skill" (p. 91). In the area of host culture characteristics, she includes such things as "less exposure to events that promote cultural questioning vs. more exposure to events that promote cultural questioning [questioning one's own as well as the host culture]" (pp. 91–92). For program characteristics and personnel, she posits such factors as "shorter program vs. longer program," and "living arrangements with other foreigners vs. living arrangements with host nationals" (p. 93). The specific variables in each area are less important for us than the notion that outcomes of study abroad are affected by the "synergistic relationship within the thematic triad" (p. 93). Similar to the more familiar (e.g., Astin, 1977) Input-Environment-Output model, Stephenson's "thematic triad" asserts that the educational outcomes of study abroad, which for Stephenson are subsumed under the concept of cross-cultural deepening, are influenced by the intersection of individual characteristics with the environment.

Rodman and Merrill's (2010) contribution is to provide a framework for understanding how the program design component of Stephenson's (2002) thematic triad comes to be. For Rodman and Merrill, macro-level influences include broad social, economic, and political influences. Mezzo influences include those pressures and factors affecting higher education more specifically. Examples include increasing tuition, changing demographics, and the accountability movement. Micro-level influences are those peculiar to an individual institution, its students, and its faculty and particularly to the vision and energy of individual leaders at that institution. Rodman and Merrill argue that program design is a product of how the factors at these three levels interact at a particular time and place. In much the same way that Pascarella (1985) uncovered the way that specific differences in institutional type, mission, environment, and context shaped student experiences, Rodman and Merrill (2010) highlight the notion that the type of study abroad program matters. Furthermore, the types of study abroad programs are a function of societal, higher education, and institutional forces.

Finally, Paulsen and St. John's (2002) student choice model will be employed as a framework to help us think about who studies abroad and who does not. We will elaborate on this model in our chapter on who studies abroad.

Sources

As mentioned earlier, the literature on study abroad is widely dispersed. Multiple contributors have extended the bibliography "Research and Literature on U.S. Students Abroad to 1987" begun by Henry Weaver (1989): (Biscarra, n.d.; Comp, n.d.a; Comp, n.d.b). The Forum on Education Abroad has recently published a comprehensive two-volume history (Hoffa, 2007; Hoffa and DePaul, 2010) that also discusses some contemporary issues. We examined the articles and data contained therein and on the websites of the major professional organizations promoting study abroad, most specifically IIE, the Council on International Educational Exchange (CIEE), and more recently the Forum on Education Abroad; academic databases, and journals. The Forum on Education Abroad publishes *Frontiers: The Interdisciplinary Journal of Study Abroad,* dedicated to research about study abroad. Our focus is primarily on studies published since 2000, although to establish a baseline we will examine some research published prior to that date. Grounded in this extensive literature foundation, we focus on the works that are most relevant and meaningful to the topics considered with an attempt to inform the readers with rich and insightful information concerning research and practice on study abroad in the United States.

The literature on study abroad poses an interesting challenge. The master narrative running through public discussion (and much research) of study abroad is one of heroic motives (international understanding, global citizenry) and glowingly beneficial outcomes for students, institutions, and participating countries. Much of the literature on some topics, for example, histories of study abroad, is written or commissioned by past leaders of the major organizations promoting study abroad such as IIE and CIEE, by leaders of professional associations such as the Forum on Education Abroad, or institutional study abroad directors. These histories often do not critique the larger national interests served by study abroad and some if its sponsors, such as IIE and CIEE. As we discuss later, many of the studies of outcomes suffer from significant methodological weaknesses.

Audience

This monograph primarily targets faculty and administrators interested in better understanding study abroad and its outcomes. Researchers interested in conducting further qualitative or quantitative research on the topic may find this monograph useful as well. This includes scholars, program administrators, students, and policymakers who have an interest in shaping the future of study abroad in the United States. While this monograph is targeted to study abroad program administrators, it may also be of interest to researchers of general education and cocurricular programs that support the general education experience.

Author Experiences with Study Abroad

To aid in understanding our approach to study abroad in the pages that follow, it is important to make explicit our own experiences with study abroad. Among us, Shannon Tumanut has the most traditional study abroad experience. As a junior at Mills College, she studied abroad for a year in France through a program offered by Academic Programs Abroad. Although not a French major when she left the United States, she credits her study abroad experience with her decision to become one. Although Mark Salisbury did not study abroad, he has spent the past few years deeply engrossed in the literature and in conducting research on study abroad. His interest in this area is formed by his experiences as a student at an undergraduate institution where most students did study abroad, his experiences working with international students, and his involvement with the Wabash National Study of Liberal Arts Education. Through these experiences he gained an understanding of how cross-cultural learning experiences affect students in important ways. Susan Twombly's first experience with study abroad came when she, as a newly promoted associate professor, decided to do a yearlong sabbatical leave at the University of Costa Rica, resulting in a study of women's experiences studying abroad. There she was confronted with many of the same experiences as the numerous U.S. study abroad students she encountered in her daily activities at and around the university. The Costa Rica experience has resulted in numerous return trips with groups of teachers and a Fulbright Fellowship to Ecuador. Collectively, our experiences have made us critical advocates for study abroad.

Definitions: Study Abroad—What It Is and What It Is Not

In the United States there is a long tradition of studying in foreign lands, and the formal and informal ways in which students have done so are varied. Since colonial times, students have gone abroad to learn languages and cultural refinement, to better themselves, to earn degrees, to engage in service and missionary work, to meet with and converse with university students from other countries, and, beginning in the twentieth century, to earn credits toward their U.S. degree.

For much of the twentieth century, study abroad was synonymous with the junior year abroad. As Heisel and Stableski (2009) note, "In its earlier form— the junior year abroad—study abroad generally was defined as a sojourn for students majoring in the humanities and the arts to perfect language skills and to gain valuable first-hand experience with the cultural artifacts and achievements of Western Europe" (p. 32). Over the course of the twentieth century, the term *study abroad* has taken on a very specific meaning that can be distinguished from the broader term *education abroad*. The Forum on Education Abroad defines education abroad as simply "education that occurs outside the participant's home country" (Forum on Education Abroad, 2011). The Forum adds that *study* abroad "results in progress toward an academic degree" (Forum on Education Abroad, 2011). IIE defines study abroad and the individuals who do it even more specifically as "U.S. citizens and permanent residents who received academic credit at their U.S. home institution for study in another country" (Chow, 2010). The key to this definition, also seen in the Forum's glossary, is receiving credit at a home U.S. institution that is used toward a degree from a U.S. college or university. It excludes U.S. students pursuing an academic degree at a non-U.S. institution as well as international students working on a degree at a U.S. university who study abroad. This definition has become industry standard to no small degree because it is the definition used by IIE as the backbone of its yearly status report on study abroad: *Open Doors*. With its focus on credits and degrees, this definition suggests a set of outcomes focused on and related to degree attainment, such as language learning and cultural competence. In other words, study abroad is not merely for personal development but is a part of and complementary to the academic degree.

In the changing context of U.S. educational objectives, degree requirements, and expectations of students and parents, this definition may undergo revision to meet the demands of a twenty-first-century education. In fact, individual institutional definitions suggest that the traditional definition may already be broadening. For example, the University of Wisconsin states that "[s]tudy abroad programs are all educational programs that take place outside the geographical boundaries of the United States. This includes both credit and noncredit programs" (University of Wisconsin, n.d.). Whereas the official IIE definition stipulates that official study abroad involves credit toward a U.S. degree, it appears that the University of Wisconsin opens the door to noncredit options for study abroad. Another relevant and recent expansion involves the boundary question (study abroad vs. study away)—can a student make gains in cross-cultural awareness without crossing an international border? Would a semester in Appalachia be more effective for a student from Seattle than a semester in Vancouver, British Columbia? The focus of this monograph, however, is on the IIE definition of study abroad, on programs that provide U.S. citizens and permanent residents with the opportunity to earn U.S. academic credit toward their U.S. degree for study in another country. We acknowledge, however, that in a changing world with increasing global mobility, it is not only possible but may be highly desirable that the IIE definition of study abroad may expand in coming years.

It is also important to note that there are groups of students who study abroad but who do so for other purposes than to complement a degree from a U.S. university: those who do so independently, those who direct enroll on their own in a university or program abroad, and those who engage in other types of educational experiences abroad, such as work, missionary and service, research, or internships (Bhandari, 2009). These groups of students are beyond the focus of this monograph.

Globalization, Internationalization, and Study Abroad

Study abroad exists within a broader framework of globalization and the internationalized university. Because these terms are used frequently, often without much elaboration, it is important to place study abroad within this larger, fluid, definitional field. To this end, Knight defines *globalization* as "the flow of technology, economy, knowledge, people, values, [and] ideas . . . across borders" (Knight and DeWit, 1997, in Knight, 2004, p. 8). We see globalization as the larger context or macro-level force in which internationalization of universities is promoted or almost demanded.[2] Although it is not the purpose of this monograph to delve deeply into the meaning of globalization in relation to study abroad, it seems accurate to say that for the most part, study abroad advocates cast globalization as a simple reality that influences how we must prepare students. Few scholars problematize the concept to ask what it means to provide study abroad in a globalized world (see, for example, Grünzweig and Rinehart, 2002). For example, what do outcomes such as *global understanding* or *global competency* mean in the face of globalization?

Knight (2004) defines *internationalization* as more than a set of activities offered by an institution to include "the process of integrating an international, intercultural or global dimension into the purpose, functions or delivery of post-secondary education" (Knight, 2003, in Knight, 2004, p. 11). Study abroad is typically one of the key mechanisms or activities institutions use to work toward the broader goal of internationalization of their campuses.

Arum (1987) casts activities such as study abroad as a subset of international exchange. International exchange "involves U.S. students and faculty studying, teaching and doing research abroad and foreign faculty and students studying, teaching and doing research in the U.S." (Arum, 1987, p. 13). Other mechanisms commonly used to foster internationalization are infusion of international courses, topics, or themes in or across the curriculum; bringing international students to the U.S. institution; institutional linkages; faculty research; and exchanges and branch campuses. Study abroad, then, as defined by IIE, is a major component of international exchange that serves as a vehicle for internationalizing a campus and meeting educational needs in a globalized world. By adopting the IIE definition of study abroad we are by no means suggesting that that is the only way of defining the study abroad experience. Clearly the experience has different meanings for institutions or individuals who participate or the families, institutions, and countries that host them.

In subsequent sections we discuss a brief history and purposes of study abroad, examine the types of programs and providers, review the research on who studies abroad (and who does not), examine outcomes of study abroad, reflect on some of the critical perspectives on study abroad, and conclude by suggesting a direction for study abroad to reach its educational potential in the next century.

History and Purposes of Study Abroad

I N ORDER TO UNDERSTAND participation in and outcomes of study abroad in the twenty-first century it is important to set study abroad in a larger historical context. As our guiding conceptual framework suggests, study abroad outcomes are a product of individual participants, the nature of programs, and the study abroad experience itself. Over time, larger political, economic, and cultural forces have interacted with trends affecting higher education and specific institutional characteristics to shape the nature and purposes of study abroad more broadly and of a program at an institution specifically. Historically, U.S. colleges have made decisions about whether and what kinds of programs to offer, and students have made decisions about whether to participate in study abroad in this larger context. A brief overview of the history of study abroad helps to provide this larger context within which to understand study abroad today. Our intent is not to repeat Hoffa's (2007) and Hoffa and DePaul's (2010) excellent and comprehensive two-volume history of study abroad published by the Forum on Education Abroad. Readers who want more historical detail are encouraged to seek out this history, which will surely become the field standard.

Study abroad has served various purposes for the larger society, for institutions, and for individual participants at different times in its relatively short history as an organized educational activity. Hoffa and DePaul (2010) argue that four main rationales or purposes have been advanced for colleges and universities to provide study abroad and for students to participate. These purposes are "the curricular argument, the cross-cultural argument, the career enhancement argument, and the development argument" (p. 8). These rationales or purposes have often overlapped. Briefly, the curricular argument is that study abroad enhances education through experiences not available on the home campus such as foreign language fluency and cross-cultural learning. Ironically the growth and success of U.S. higher education itself may weaken this rationale (Hoffa and DePaul, 2010). That is, it may be hard for U.S. students to see benefits of studying abroad in their own increasingly professionally oriented programs of study when the U.S. system of higher education is touted as the best in the world.

The cross-cultural rationale "contends that study abroad provides U.S. students with a unique opportunity to learn about their own 'Americanness,' to understand a foreign culture more deeply through immersion, or to witness the emerging global culture" (Hoffa and DePaul, 2010, p. 9). The career enhancement rationale directly speaks to the argument that skills developed through study abroad are valued in the workplace both at home and in an increasingly global marketplace. Finally, the student development rationale speaks to the long-standing belief that study abroad contributes to social, emotional, and intellectual development (Hoffa and DePaul, 2010). More specifically, the growing investment and emphasis at both the federal and institutional level on increasing study abroad participation turns on the popular and long-accepted belief that a study abroad experience uniquely improves the intercultural skills of all participants (Commission on the Abraham Lincoln Study Abroad Fellowship Program, 2005; NAFSA, 2003; National Task Force on Undergraduate Education Abroad, 1990). Hoffa and DePaul, 2010, (and Gore, 2005) note that these various rationales (e.g., study abroad for fun, adventure or personal exploration) often compete with or work at cross-purposes to the status of study abroad as serious academic work. Moreover, there has not always been agreement about the purposes of study abroad. Specifically, study abroad traditionalists who see the primary purpose of study abroad as academic, and immersion programs as the program of choice, have not always agreed with those who give priority to the career, skills, student development rationales and who are more accepting of newer, shorter-term study abroad programs (Hoffa, 2007). Today, as our review will show, global competency and global understanding are seen as almost necessary for college graduates, although there is no consensus on what such outcomes mean.

From the national perspective, the broad goal for organized study abroad can be, and has been, framed as promoting world understanding; spreading the good word about the United States (culture, democracy); promoting world peace and understanding; economic competitiveness; and, depending on one's point of view, national security or even imperialism. And, finally, the purposes of study abroad for colleges and universities themselves have become more salient as study abroad has become a major vehicle for internationalizing colleges and universities. Institutional purposes include study abroad as a vehicle for internationalization of campus and curriculum, as a means of attracting students and providing them with engaging educational activities as well as providing a source of income (source) and rankings. These various purposes will become evident through our brief review.

Beginnings

Crossing borders to study in other countries or cultures is as old as higher education itself (Hoffa, 2007; Lucas, 2006). The U.S. tradition of study abroad as an institutionally sponsored, group activity is generally traced to professors at several late-nineteenth-century eastern colleges who conducted "groups of young ladies on educational tours of Europe, visiting museums, cathedrals and the like" (Bowman, 1987, p. 13), the female version of the European Grand Tour through which young people learned language, culture, and connections through travel.[3] The first organized study abroad programs, then, emerged post World War I in a few eastern colleges as organized opportunities largely for female students to travel abroad. Two types of early programs dominated: the Junior Year Abroad (JYA) and faculty-led study tours, often on ships (Hoffa, 2007). The purposes of the JYA were curricular (to develop foreign language skills); cross-cultural (to learn about other cultures as a means of preventing future wars); and developmental, through an academic year immersed in one country. The study tour was often shorter in duration and led by U.S. faculty members. The typical study tour visited several countries with the purpose of learning about those countries, and conducted classes in English. The JYA and the study tour were promoted by passionate faculty members with an international vision. Institutions also began to develop short-term programs for specific majors (Hoffa, 2007) during this interwar period. Hoffa (2007) cites Georgetown and Indiana University as among early leaders in short-term programs.

Several critical factors coincided in the interwar period to establish study abroad as a group program tied to a U.S. college degree. First, the elective system that broke apart the old prescribed liberal arts education became widely accepted in the early twentieth century. This was accompanied by the credit system for recognizing academic work (Hoffa, 2007; Lucas, 2006). A college degree became an accumulation of credits toward a major and electives rather than completion of a prescribed curriculum (Hoffa, 2007). In addition, the emergence of general education, deans of men and women, and residence halls signaled a continued and expanded institutional concern for the growth and development of the whole student (Lucas, 2006), which Bowman (1987) argues resulted in Americans' preferences for organized group study abroad programs. Undoubtedly, other factors, such as a growing middle class (Levine, 1986) with an interest in Europe, the League of Nations, and other postwar efforts to foster cultural understanding and peace contributed to an interest in U.S. study abroad (Hoffa, 2007).

Individual campus study abroad efforts received a major boost from the founding of the Institute of International Education in 1919. The IIE was the first of a series of influential independent nonprofit, nongovernmental national organizations to play a critical role in promoting study abroad in the United States (Hoffa, 2007). The IIE founders "believed that we [the U.S.] could not achieve lasting peace without greater understanding between nations—and that international educational exchange formed the strongest basis for fostering such understanding" (IIE, n.d.c).

The new IIE engaged in several critical activities. It created the Committee on the Junior Year Abroad, recommended policies to ensure quality of junior year abroad programs, and served to fill an important gap mediating between government policies and colleges and universities, particularly with respect to admitting students from abroad to U.S. universities, which was much of IIE's early focus. IIE quickly became involved in promoting internationalism in higher education by serving as a clearinghouse for curricular and practice information (Hoffa, 2007) and in so doing advocated for study abroad to become part of the undergraduate curriculum rather than an extracurricular activity. As a result of these factors, some U.S. colleges began to recognize that international consciousness—and study abroad—ought to be part of the formal curriculum (e.g., a credit-bearing activity) through the three forms mentioned earlier: the JYA, faculty-led study tours such as those provided by the University Travel Association on ships, and summer study.

Post–World War II

With the end of World War II, study abroad, which had stopped during the war, slowly resumed. Curricular rationales for study abroad can be seen in expanding types of study abroad programs to include not only the traditional JYA programs and faculty-led study tours but programs such as faculty-organized exchanges and tutorials, dissertation research abroad, institutes for foreign students organized by foreign universities, customized forms of the JYA, U.S. college branch campuses in foreign countries, short-term study abroad organized either by a U.S. college or university or by a non-college-based organization (for example, the American Institute for Foreign Study, Semester at Sea), and consortia of colleges banding together to offer study abroad (Hoffa, 2007).

The devastation caused by the war and the rise of the Cold War brought the federal government into a greater role in educational exchange and study abroad (Bu, 1999). The federal government promoted several acts and initiatives in this period that encouraged study abroad. Among them were the Fulbright Program; the Smith-Mundt Act (1948), which linked educational exchange with information dissemination; the National Defense Education Act (1957), which promoted language and area studies specialists; the Foreign Assistance Act, which established the U.S. Agency for International Development and the Peace Corps; and the State Department Bureau of Educational and Cultural Affairs, which provided subsidies to establish study abroad programs in Latin America (Hoffa, 2007).

Study abroad took on added importance beyond its educational function. As Mikhailova (2002) notes, regardless of motive, students were ambassadors who could "represent the best national interests of American society and promote international understanding" (p. 1). A number of national and federal programs and organizations became promoters of study abroad—and as Bu (1999) argues—contractors for the U.S. government and its postwar foreign policy objectives. Among the most notable and influential such programs and organizations were the Fulbright International Education Exchange Program, CIEE, and the National Association of Foreign Student Affairs (NAFSA).

Although it does not directly support study abroad, the Fulbright Program has been a major force in promoting international scholarly exchange of U.S. and foreign university faculty members who then integrate international content into their teaching and research. CIEE has played a major role as provider of information and travel opportunities and promoter of standards (Mikhailova, 2002, p. 4). CIEE remains one of the principal organizations promoting and supporting study abroad through programs, advocacy, and knowledge creation (CIEE, n.d.). Founded in 1947 as an organization for administrators who worked with foreign students in U.S. colleges and universities, NAFSA has recently emerged as a major national professional organization concerned with the professional development of study abroad administrators. IIE took on new and important functions after World War II. In 1954 it began publication of its now annual Open Doors Report, funded by the U.S. Department of State to track the flow of students into and out of the United States for college-level study.

In the Cold War period, educational exchange was seen as one means of diplomacy or national security (Bu, 1999). Bu (1999) says, "With the government taking the lead in promoting educational and cultural exchanges, the programs began to be broadly integrated with political goals and foreign policy deliberations" (p. 397). This was most obvious in faculty exchange programs sponsored by the U.S. Agency for International Development, World Bank, Fulbright, IIE, Ford Foundation, and CIEE involving grant money targeted to specific countries and with specific objectives, but it was also evident in the rationale for supporting study abroad programs in places such as Central America (Bu, 1999; Hoffa, 2007). This is not to say that U.S. college faculty readily accepted the often covert diplomatic purposes of educational exchange and study abroad. Bu argues that especially government-sponsored study abroad has existed in tension between Americanizing others, spreading American values and more honestly pure educational values. Recognizing these tensions, educators have often resisted being used as instruments in the war against Communism or U.S. foreign policy in general (and still do; Bu, 1999; Hoffa, 2007).

Of efforts to count participation before 1965, Hoffa (2007) writes, "While the precise numbers of programs and undergraduate students abroad during the early 1960s is almost impossible to determine, the demographics of Open Doors combined with the more informal tabulations of [other studies] makes it abundantly clear that overseas study by U.S. students was steadily growing" (p. 235).

Study Abroad Post-Vietnam

During the period from 1965 to the present, study abroad has been dominated by two trends: greater access (accompanied by tremendous growth) and academic legitimation (Hoffa and DePaul, 2010). The Vietnam War, the fall of the Berlin Wall, end of the Cold War, 9/11, and globalization all influenced study abroad in this period. Higher education experienced tremendous growth accompanied by increased emphasis on education as a private good, on research, and more recently, a renewed emphasis on undergraduate learning. Over this span of time, a new rationale for study abroad emerged: developing competencies for successfully competing in a globalized world.

The past twenty years have been shaped by persistent efforts to internationalize campuses and students driven by such organizations as the American Council on Education, the American Association of Colleges and Universities, and the Forum on Education Abroad, a voluntary membership organization formed in 2000 to promote research, programming, and standards in study abroad (Forum on Education Abroad, n.d.). The period is marked by a diversification of study abroad in a variety of aspects to include new forms of study abroad to accommodate majors previously not targeted for study abroad (DeWinter and Rumbley, 2010), diversification of participating students (Stallman, Woodruff, Kasravi, and Comp, 2010), and geographic locations to include developing nations as well as the well-established European destinations (Ogden, Soneson, and Weting, 2010). Shorter study abroad options have become more plentiful and popular to accommodate packed curricula and busy and financially strapped students. The Higher Education Assistance Act of 1965 gave institutions the ability to allow students to use financial aid for study abroad (Hoffa, 2007), and more recent federal legislation made federal financial aid explicitly available for study abroad. The Gilman International Scholarship was established in 2000 to provide scholarships for Pell grant recipients (Bolen, 2001, p. 185). These efforts have facilitated diversification of student participants. In particular, community colleges have been a relatively new entrant in the study abroad world. In 2008–2009 a reported 5,327 community college students studied abroad, about 2 percent of the total U.S. students who studied abroad that year (IIE, 2010). Even though a relatively small number, it marks a significant shift in the study abroad population.

Organizational Advocacy for Study Abroad in a Post-9/11 World

The post-9/11 period has been marked by concerted efforts to internationalize colleges and universities and to promote study abroad.[4] Because much of the current rationale for study abroad is informed directly by these efforts, we provide a more detailed account of them. In the wake of the 9/11 attacks on the World Trade Center and the Pentagon, the American Council on Education (ACE) published *Beyond September 11: A Comprehensive National Policy on International Education* (2002), urgently calling on the federal government to reverse decades of declining emphasis on international education and foreign language study and instill new national policy that would prioritize international education. *Beyond September 11* merely continued advocacy for study abroad and foreign language acquisition begun in the 1980s and 1990s (Cornwell and Stoddard, 1999; Johnston and Edelstein, 1993; National Task Force on Undergraduate Education Abroad, 1990; President's Commission on Foreign Languages and International Study, 1980). Educators and politicians were joined by business leaders who argued that college graduates with internationally compatible skills such as second language fluency and knowledge of international cultures and customs would be vital to the continued profitability of the firm and, by extension, the nation (Adelman, 1994; Bikson and Law, 1994).

Since 2001, increasing the number of college graduates with the ability to effectively interact internationally has emerged as a national policy priority (APLU, 2004; Commission on the Abraham Lincoln Study Abroad Fellowship Program, 2005; Senator Paul Simon Foundation Act of 2007, HR 1469/S. 991). With the National Commission on Terrorist Attacks Upon the United States (the 9/11 Commission, 2003), which bemoaned the small number of college graduates with degrees in Arabic studies, as a backdrop, the recommendations of NAFSA's Strategic Task Force on Education Abroad (2003), and the efforts of its honorary co-chair Senator Paul Simon, Congress appropriated funds in 2003 to create the Commission on the Abraham Lincoln Study Abroad Fellowship Program (Consolidated Appropriations Act, 2004). The goal of this commission was to find ways in which the federal government might facilitate a substantial increase in annual study abroad participation. President George W. Bush declared 2006 "The Year of Study Abroad." Soon thereafter the Higher Education Reconciliation Act of 2005 created the National Sciences and Mathematics Access to Retain Talent (SMART) Grants that included scholarship funds for students majoring in foreign languages deemed critical to national security interests (Deficit Reduction Act of 2005, 2005).

The efforts of the Lincoln Commission represented bold aspirations to make study abroad a more central piece of the undergraduate experience. The Commission's report (2005) established an ambitious goal of one million American students studying abroad annually by 2016–2017. The Commission proposed that Congress appropriate annual funding of $50 million initially, with incremental increases to reach $125 million annually by 2011–2012 to fund nonrenewable scholarships of up to $5,000 to pay the costs of studying abroad. The Lincoln Commission especially encouraged participation among traditionally underrepresented populations and proposed criteria that would ensure quality control in the study abroad programs supported by this effort. Finally, the Commission proposed that higher education institutions partner with the federal government by increasing their own investment in study abroad scholarships in response to this federal initiative so that federal dollars could be most efficiently used to encourage study abroad growth across all types of postsecondary institutions.

Despite almost universal support for study abroad, the resulting legislation, titled The Senator Paul Simon Study Abroad Foundation Act of 2007 (2007) has struggled to survive the lawmaking process in the face of recent grim economic realities. Nonetheless, the broad public support for study abroad generated by the Lincoln Commission helped to further galvanize higher education organizations on behalf of international education generally and study abroad in particular (Blum, 2006; Chmela, 2005; Farrell, 2007). For example, throughout the past decade, ACE has sponsored an extensive series of programs and publications to promote internationalization among higher education institutions through its Center for International Initiatives, emphasizing the investment institutions should make in supporting study abroad participation (ACE 2008; Field, 2009; Green, 2005; Green, Luu, and Burris, 2008; Hill and Green, 2008; Olson, Green, and Hill, 2005, 2006; Siaya and Hayward, 2003).

At the same time, the AAC&U Liberal Learning and America's Promise (LEAP; AAC&U, 2007) initiative further situated study abroad as an ideal means of developing one of the central educational outcomes of a liberal arts education—intercultural knowledge and competence. Study abroad participation was highlighted as an example of an educational experience that would positively influence gains in each of the four categories of outcomes deemed critical for a liberally educated person: knowledge of human cultures and the physical and natural world, intellectual and practical skills, personal and social responsibility, and integrative learning. In 2008 the AAC&U further emphasized the value of study abroad participation in *High Impact Educational Practices: What They Are, Who Has Access to Them, and Why They Matter* (Kuh, 2008). Study abroad was prominently featured as one such activity. Institutions were further encouraged to support and promote study abroad participation, especially for students with few prior cross-cultural experiences.

The growing chorus of public and private support for the importance of study abroad has resulted in continued growth in institutional support and student participation. Reporting data from an ACE survey of internationalization efforts at higher education institutions, Siaya and Hayward (2003) noted comparative increases over the previous decade in the proportion of institutions that administered study abroad programs and the proportion of institutions that provided financial support for students participating in those programs. ACE followed up these findings five years later and found that the proportion of institutions administering study abroad programs had increased again—85 percent in 2003 to 91 percent in 2008 (Green, Luu, and Burris, 2008). Moreover, despite the economic recession that followed 9/11 and the accompanying American fears of travel or studying abroad (Borcover, 2002; McKeown, 2003; Siaya and Hayward, 2003), the compound annual growth rate of study abroad participation between 2002 and 2007 was 8.48 percent—only minimally less than the 8.91 percent compound annual growth rate between 1997 and 2002 (National Center for Education Statistics [NCES], 2008a, 2008b)—with the absolute number of study abroad participants growing from 174,629 in 2002–2003 to 262,416 in 2007–2008.

Societal and Institutional Purposes of Study Abroad in the Twenty-First Century

In the twenty-first century, diplomatic, foreign policy, and national security purposes so prominent in the Cold War period, if present at all, seem to have taken a backseat to economic ones. Today the rationale for study abroad from the federal government and business community has shifted from diplomacy and national security to a largely economic rationale: competitiveness in a global market. Even 9/11 did not seem to shift the rhetorical landscape from commerce to national security, although there clearly is a relationship between the two. To keep the United States in a world leadership role, political and business leaders—and educators—argue that students must have the knowledge and skills to function in a global world. As former president Clinton noted, "To continue to compete successfully in a global economy and to maintain our role as a world leader, the United States needs to ensure that its citizens develop a broad understanding of the world, proficiency in other languages, and knowledge of other cultures" (Clinton, 2000, in Bolen, 2001, p. 186). To accomplish this, "federal financial aid, government policy, and study abroad advocates have joined together in the past decade [1990s] to create a mass market for American exchange programs" (Bolen, 2001, p. 185), and the variety of programs facilitate it. In other words, higher education associations as well as colleges and universities are willing participants in supporting the economic rationale and for the parallel commodification of study abroad (Zemach-Bersin, 2009).

From the institutional perspective, study abroad has taken on a life of its own. As indicated earlier, study abroad is one of the key ways of internationalizing the campus. Recently, with the publication and widespread use of the National Survey of Student Engagement, institutions have found an ally that supports study abroad as a means of engaging students in academic pursuits that directly relates to retention and graduation rates. Study abroad in the twenty-first century fits well with Brint's (2011) description of the new progressivism in higher education that emphasizes a renewed emphasis on teaching, most specifically on "active learning, civic engagement and sensitivity to the interests of diverse learners" (p. 46).

The more idealistic, missionary-like goals (world peace) of early study abroad proponents have been replaced by rationales rooted in individual and institutional payoff. In this consumer-oriented higher education environment, study abroad has become a way for institutions to market themselves (Bolen, 2001; Engle and Engle, 2003; Zemach-Bersin, 2009). One can hardly find a college website that does not foreground the institutions' global or international nature, including opportunities for its current and future students to study abroad. They do so for very good reasons. Cressey and Stubbs (2010) report data showing that 80 percent of college-going students and their parents consider having an international dimension to be important in their college search.

This vision of study abroad is not without its critics. Bolen (2001) and Zemach-Bersin (2007, 2009) argue that the phenomenal growth in the number of students studying abroad accompanies prepackaged programs that can be likened to consumer experiences: housing, food, adventure, tours, orientation, with courses added. From this perspective, short-term programs in particular provide instant culture without students having to sacrifice too much or work too hard. Study abroad is a consumable, more like educational tourism than a true educational experience and is frequently advertised as such (Zemach-Bersin, 2009). In addition, students now have expectations of linking study abroad to job opportunities. In this view, study abroad is not just something to be experienced for personal growth and development but is related to specific career outcomes (much like most of liberal education itself). A story about the results of a recent IES Abroad study of its study abroad graduates only confirms this by headlining the fact that survey respondents who studied abroad were more likely to obtain career-related jobs earlier and to make more money than graduates who had not studied abroad (PRWeb, 2012). The danger of such commodification of study abroad as tourist experience is that without strong study abroad programs providing authentic study abroad experiences, ". . . it is ironic that Americans could easily become 'the new provincials,' rich and powerful, yet culturally impoverished by the illusions of national self-sufficiency" (Falk and Kanach, 2000, p. 167).

Finally, study abroad participation rates have become yet an indicator of institutional prestige. IIE lists on its Open Door web page links to lists of the leading institutions for total students studying abroad, for study abroad by institutional type, for study abroad by duration, and for undergraduate participation rates (IIE, n.d.d). Such reports are both a recognition that study abroad is a legitimate educational activity and a potential curse. Our purpose here is not to discuss and critique the college ranking literature. However, it is clear that rankings can encourage institutions to engage in practices valued by rankings (for example, getting as many students as possible to study abroad). The effect of rankings on institutional behavior with respect to study abroad is not clear at this point.

Summary

Study abroad in the United States has developed as an institutional activity, providing students the opportunity to earn part of a degree by studying in another country for a year or shorter terms. From modest beginnings as chaperoned study for women, today study abroad programs of various kinds, fields of study, and durations can be found in almost any country or region of the world, including Antarctica. The top four destinations remain European. Over the past twenty years, the number of U.S. students studying abroad has more than quadrupled from about 55,000 in 1989–1990 to slightly over 270,000 in 2009–2010 (IIE, 2011). By 2008, more than 90 percent of all colleges and universities in the United States had study abroad programs (Green, Luu, and Burris, 2008; Hoffa and DePaul, 2010). This growth has been prompted by the efforts of major higher education associations, the business community, and the federal government and has been accompanied by calls for standards and evidence of outcomes. In addition, organizations such as IIE and CIEE continue to promote study abroad, and the major educational associations have taken an active role in promoting study abroad as a means to achieving critical learning outcomes and thereby for promoting the important national goal of preparing globally competent citizens who can compete in the global marketplace.

Types of Programs and Providers

T HE INCREASE IN THE NUMBER of students studying abroad has been made possible in part by an expansion in the types of study abroad programs offered. Rodman and Merrill (in Hoffa and DePaul, 2010) describe the number and types of study abroad programs as "a veritable exhibit hall containing thousands of individual, inventive and original models" (p. 199), a reference, no doubt, to the annual NAFSA conference in which more than 400 institutions, organizations, and other service providers distribute information about their many different programs and services to conference attendees (NAFSA, n.d.). No longer is the "junior year abroad" the only, or even the most popular, form of study abroad. In fact, the most recent IIE data indicate that 57 percent of all study abroad students in 2009–2010 engaged in short-term programs (eight weeks or less), another 39 percent engaged in mid-length programs (a semester or less), and only 4 percent participated in long-term programs (an academic year or longer) (IIE, 2011). The default assumption that study abroad must last for a prescribed amount of time is now defunct, and the popularity of short-term programs such as those that occur over institutions' spring or winter breaks or study abroad embedded in existing home-institution courses has risen considerably (Hochhauser, 2005; Stallman, Woodruff, Kasravi, and Comp, 2010; Zachrisson, 2005). Because of the explosion of program types, it makes little sense to describe current types in great detail. Rather, we will focus on common ways of describing and categorizing study abroad programs and providers. Readers interested in more detailed descriptions are referred to the Forum on Education Abroad's glossary (Forum on Education Abroad, 2011).

There have been various attempts to make some sense out of the plethora of study abroad program types. These attempts seem to fall into two general approaches to classifying programs. The first is descriptive and typically classifies programs based on one primary explicit characteristic of the program, such as length or location. The second type of classification scheme is more analytic and is based on multiple dimensions or critical components of programs, such as length of stay, degree of immersion, degree of structure, language of instruction, or housing arrangements.

Descriptive, Single-Component Schemes

Until World War II there were typically three main types of study abroad programs: the Junior Year Abroad; faculty-led study tours; and short-term, campus-sponsored programs. In the latter half of the twentieth century, study abroad diversified considerably to include by some accounts up to seventeen different types of programs (Hoffa, 2007).

IIE, the major data gatherer and reporter on study abroad, currently categorizes study abroad programs simply by duration: short-term, mid-length, and long-term. IIE further defines short-term as any program taking place in the summer, midsemester, or for eight weeks or less during the academic year (IIE, 2011). Mid-length programs are equivalent to a quarter (or two) or a semester abroad, and long-term are programs of an academic or calendar year in duration. Again, IIE records only for-credit experiences and does not record work experiences or other kinds of learning experiences for which students do not receive academic credit at their home institution. The IIE scheme makes no attempt to consider program focus, goals, or nature of student experience. This has prompted others to develop more descriptive classification frameworks typically based on program structure.

The Forum on Education Abroad has created a current typology of program types based on the type of student experience. According to this classification, programs fall into the following categories: field study programs (experiential study outside of the classroom such as service learning and field biology programs), integrated university study (participation is predominantly in regular courses provided by the host university and offered primarily for host-university students), overseas branch campus (U.S. college or university with branch in a foreign country), study abroad center (classroom based with courses designed for study abroad students), and travel seminar (students travel from country to country) (Forum on Education Abroad, 2011).

The Forum's glossary goes on to list twenty-four common descriptors used for various programs and subtypes. Some of the most commonly used descriptors for program types include academic internship program, bilateral student exchange (typically involves exchange of students), direct enrollment program (study at overseas university with no formal assistance of a program provider), faculty-led program (led and directed by a faculty member from home campus, usually short duration), immersion program (emphasis is on integrating U.S. students into host culture), hybrid program (combines several program types), customized program, area studies program (focus is on studying a region), island program (U.S. students typically live and study together), language institutes (programs often run by universities or organizations in the host country for language study), embedded program (study abroad is embedded as a component of a home-based course), and service-learning program (focus is on field study that serves needs of a community) (Forum on Education Abroad, 2011). Reviewing the types of programs listed by NAFSA over the years, Rodman and Merrill (2010) identify recent types of study abroad options that go beyond the traditional: independent study, field study/ experiential programs, and various types of work abroad. The work category abroad includes for credit and not-for-credit.

These kinds of classification schemes are problematic for a number of reasons. First, although these categories are often portrayed as discrete, it is probably more accurate to describe them as a list of potentially significant aspects of a study abroad program. Yet the way that these classifications are often utilized, they seem to function as exclusive descriptors of programs when a given study abroad program may in fact combine a variety of these programmatic aspects (Engle and Engle, 2003; Vande Berg, n.d.). For example, a program could be listed as either short-term or direct enrollment when in fact it could be both. A study center program could be short term or long term, taught in the target language or not, by U.S. or host-country faculty. Furthermore, these classification schema are not particularly adaptable to the seemingly steady state of change in the study abroad landscape—the very challenge these schema attempt to address. For example, they are not able to capture fully the complexities of projects designed to integrate study abroad into the curriculum (see Brewer and Cunningham, 2009).

In addition to not accurately reflecting the complexity of experience expected in any one study abroad program, the descriptive labels say little about how a specific study abroad program configuration might impact learning uniquely. For example, using the descriptor "integrated university study" to describe a program says little about what students are expected to learn as a result. The implications for students and parents are that the shorthand descriptors may understate what students will actually do or learn. For program administrators and researchers, assessment becomes an ad hoc exercise in random investigation in the absence of specifically articulated outcomes that are intentionally designed into the program.

Multiple-Criterion Classification Schemes

Classification schemes based on multiple program dimensions deemed critical to the study abroad experience seek to overcome the limitations of the descriptive typologies by focusing on critical components and/or goals of study abroad. They allow colleges and universities and researchers to map the characteristics of programs on various program dimensions, thus capturing the diverse facets of the many program types that have emerged in recent years.

One of the earliest attempts to describe study abroad on various dimensions was provided by John Engle and Lili Engle (2003), long-time codirectors of the American University Center of Provence in Aix-en-Provence, France. Bothered by what they saw as the indiscriminate lumping of "junior year abroad programs" with short-term travel and including between-semester programs under the umbrella term of *study abroad*, Engle and Engle (2003) proposed a scheme that they argued more accurately categorizes study abroad programs. Such differentiation is essential, they argue, if we are to understand program goals and outcomes accurately.

Engle and Engle developed what they call a "level-based classification system" based on degrees of immersion and challenge. The levels of study abroad in their framework are: Level One: Study Tour; Level Two: Short-Term Study; Level Three: Cross-Cultural Contact Program; Level Four: Cross-Cultural Encounter Program; Level Five: Cross-Cultural Immersion Program (Engle and Engle, 2003, pp. 10–11). The second part of their framework consists of comparable "objective" criteria or program components: length of sojourn, entry target-language competence, language of instruction, context of academic work, types of student housing, provisions for guided social/cultural interaction, and requirements for guided reflection (p. 8). Juxtaposing levels and components against each other, Engle and Engle produce a rubric describing characteristics of programs at each level. For example, duration of a Level One study tour is several days to a few weeks, whereas duration for Level Five cross-cultural immersion programs is a semester to a year. Language for the study tour is English, whereas it is 100 percent target language for the cross-cultural immersion program. The Engle and Engle classification system is based on the assumption that the factor that distinguishes study abroad from study of the other cultures from the home campus is or should be to present "participants with a challenge—the emotional and intellectual challenge of direct, authentic cultural encounters and guided reflection on those encounters" (p. 7). Their scheme further assumes that the primary emphasis of study abroad is language and culture and thus privileges studying in countries in which English is not the native language.

Michael Vande Berg and the Forum on Education Abroad (Vande Berg, n.d.) built on the work of Engle and Engle to provide another two-dimensional framework for classifying study abroad programs. The Forum's proposed system is based on a continuum of "structured, focused opportunities to integrate culturally" on one dimension (Vande Berg, n.d.). The second dimension consists of seven components that influence student learning in study abroad. The seven components are length of stay, entry target language competence, extent to which target language is used in onsite coursework, context of academic work (who teaches and whether course is home-institution course or host-university course), type of housing, structured and guided cultural learning experiences, and on-site mentoring (Vande Berg, n.d.). Each of these can be rated on the extent to which it provides structured and focused opportunities to achieve cultural integration.

These multiple-dimension or criterion-based approaches to typing programs seem to have several advantages over the more traditional descriptive approaches. First, they recognize that any one of the traditional-type programs may fit more than one category and that the nuances of twenty-first-century study abroad programs cannot be captured by labeling programs based on one dimension only. Simply put, study abroad programs have many dimensions that cannot be captured by a single descriptive label. They also recognize that a short-term program may actually meet some of the higher-level immersion goals, whereas a yearlong program may not. As the types of programs proliferate, the chance of fitting programs into only one category declines. Second, these frameworks, of which the Engle and Engle framework seems most developed and comprehensive, have the potential to provide study abroad program sponsors with a guide to developing more sophisticated and complete statements of program characteristics and associated outcomes and participants with a more complete understanding of the goals and experiences associated with study abroad programs. Third, such frameworks seem useful and essential in helping to associate program type with effects of study abroad and/or to develop program outcomes assessment processes that make sense. They are likely no less easy to use in large-scale quantitatively based research projects.

Frameworks such as Engle and Engle's also have their limitations. For example, there may be considerable debate about the assumptions embedded in the choices of components or levels and criteria. Engle and Engle's framework seems to be based on a more traditional view of study abroad that privileges studying in non-English-speaking countries. The descriptive terms that fill in the boxes of their rubric may also be subject to criticism and debate. For example, they determine that an in-house institute for foreign students is a Level Two on context of academic work component. Vande Berg avoids this problem by not providing descriptors of program components at various stages on his continua. Moreover, such classification schemes may not have advertising appeal. These criticisms notwithstanding, such classification frameworks seem to provide an essential aid to enable institutions to provide the most useful information to students and parents and for institutions and researchers to assess the outcomes of study abroad.

Who Provides Study Abroad

There are a variety of study abroad providers. Here, too, there is considerable confusion and lack of precision of terminology. Although the accepted definition of study abroad insists that students be earning credits toward a college degree from a U.S. college or university, the programs may not be organized and run through the students' home institutions at all. Rather, students from one college or university may participate in a study abroad experience offered by another college or university (in the U.S. or abroad) or a third-party provider. Typically, the study abroad program must be approved by the student's home institution in order for credit to be given. We highlight several common organizational frameworks for providing study abroad.

- *The institutionally administered program.* These programs are developed and run by the sponsoring U.S. colleges or universities in all aspects, including control of instruction, housing, awarding of grades, and so on. A sponsoring U.S. college or university may control some aspects of the program, such as maintaining an agreement with the host institution, admissions, orientation, housing, or maintaining an on-ground staff of some sort, but not the actual instruction. Increasingly, this includes the home institution's having branch campuses or study centers in the host country.
- *Consortia of colleges to share study abroad offerings.* The Associated Colleges of the Midwest is a good example of just such a consortium. Typically these programs make their offerings available to others in the consortium, and consortium institutions agree to accept study abroad credits taken through its programs.
- *Relinquishment of study abroad programs.* Colleges and universities may cede some or all of their study abroad programs to programs established and run by other colleges and universities.
- *Foreign institutes.* Colleges and universities may grant credit for work done at a foreign-run institute (sort of the foreign version of a third-party provider).
- *Third-party providers.* Third-party providers include nongovernmental, not-for-profit organizations such as CIEE, the American Institute for Foreign Studies (AIFS), and the Institute for the International Education of

Students (IES Abroad), to name a few, while others operate with a profit motive. IIE reported that approximately one quarter of students studying abroad in 2000–2007 did so through a third-party provider (Redden, 2007b).

Colleges and universities may contract with third-party providers to offer specific programs or may simply add them to the list of approved providers from which they will accept academic credits. The AIFS website explains one way in which this occurs: "Once there is a decision to work with AIFS, affiliates distribute the AIFS catalog to interested students, facilitate the transfer of credit, invite AIFS to study abroad fairs, display posters in prominent locations, advise AIFS on potential program offerings, arrange student meetings and generally become knowledgeable about AIFS college programs" (AIFS Abroad, n.d.). AIFS has been remarkably successful, as evidenced by the fact that it has become a "$180,000,000 operation with offices in five countries and 50,000 students, travelers and clients each year" (Rodman and Merrill, 2010, p. 227). A quick Google search reveals dozens of third-party providers of study abroad programs. IES Abroad is yet another prominent nonprofit third-party provider. Its website advertises 100 study abroad and internship programs in Europe, Africa, Asia, South America, Australia, and New Zealand enrolling approximately 5,500 student from 185 U.S. colleges and universities annually (IES Abroad, n.d.). The International Partnership for Service Learning is yet another organization that offers undergraduate study abroad through service-learning programs (Tonkin, 2004).

Outside providers vary widely in the services and types of programs offered (Redden, 2007b). Reasons for using these providers include the variety in programming offered, administrative support, and ability to provide onsite support for students. These rationales are particularly salient for small colleges, some of which do not have the capacity to establish their own programs abroad or in many countries.

Of late, these private, third-party providers have come under considerable scrutiny from the press for offering perks to institutional officials who send students their way. As Redden argues (Redden, 2007a), the issue is complex.

On the one hand, it seems contrary to ethical principles for college officials to accept benefits from sending students to a third-party provider. On the other hand, study abroad is often an auxiliary service that must pay for itself, leading institutions to seek support where they can find it, although not support for individual program officer benefit.

One of the issues that the debate over third-party providers raises is that the field is growing very rapidly while it is professionalizing at the same time. There are attempts at standardizing language, terms, practices, and statements of ethical principles, as well as developing voluntary systems of accreditation, but as of yet little agreement. The various associations, such as CIEE, IIE, NAFSA, and the Forum on Education Abroad, are working toward consensus on some of these matters as we write. The Forum has developed a set of ethical principles and "best practices," but it represents only about 250 of the U.S. institutions that offer study abroad. The second issue raised by proliferation of program types and study abroad providers is standards about which the above-mentioned organizations are attempting to develop consensus. As study abroad grows in importance and the types of programs and providers proliferates, agreed-upon standards will become essential.

Summary

Since 1965 a wealth of study abroad program types has emerged in response to macroeconomic, political, and social forces that have influenced the rationale(s) for study abroad, which have in turn shaped the development of program types. Rodman and Merrill (2010) conclude that ". . . the recent history of study abroad program design is one characterized by response to *needs* and *circumstances*, in the local organizational *context*. The associated variables are effectively framed through the *vision* of individuals who possess the ability to move others to *action* (emphasis in the original; p. 200).

Various methods of describing and categorizing this plethora of programs exist. These methods may be grouped into ones based on one single defining program characteristic and those that are criterion or multicomponent based. The latter overcome some of the weaknesses of the single-component schemes and provide a more comprehensive way of understanding programs that reflect their growing complexity. These models, while perhaps too complicated for public relations purposes, offer a sounder platform for understanding outcomes of study abroad and for establishing outcomes assessment programs. Study abroad is organized and provided by institutions, foreign institutes, and consortia of colleges and universities, as well as third-party providers.

Who Studies Abroad and Who Does Not

A RGUABLY, THE PRIMARY OBJECTIVE of study abroad advocacy in recent years has focused on expanding the number of U.S. students studying abroad. At the same time, study abroad advocates have long lamented the disproportionate nature of study abroad participation rates among undergraduates (Council on International Educational Exchange [CIEE], 1991; Dessoff, 2006; Koester, 1985; Lambert, 1989; Redden, 2008). In this chapter we consider both who studies abroad (and intends to do so) and who does not and why. In particular, we examine the factors that seem to influence intent to participate and actual participation in study abroad. It is useful to reiterate here that the duration and types of study abroad programs for undergraduates have adapted to meet both the demands of an ever more diverse student body and the rising concern of institutions (and society in general) that international academic experience is essential if the aim of a more global citizenry is to be achieved (Heisel and Stableski, 2009; Whalen, 2009). It is not for lack of options that students do not study abroad.

Despite an overall increase in the number of students studying abroad, a couple of notable facts remain. The overall percentage of U.S. students who study abroad remains stubbornly below 2 percent of total U.S. undergraduates, and the profile of students who go abroad has changed relatively little over the past several decades. Typically, those who study abroad are "white, female, young, single, financially comfortable, and without disability" (Stallman, Woodruff, Kasravi, and Comp, 2010). Additionally, the most common majors of study abroad students are social sciences and humanities (Obst, Bhandari, and Witherell, 2007; Paus and Robinson, 2008; Stallman, Woodruff, Kasravi, and Comp, 2010; Stroud, 2010). Although current data show that study abroad has begun to attract and, to some extent, enroll greater numbers of underrepresented students (Brux and Fry, 2010; Obst, Bhandari, and Witherell, 2007; Stallman, Woodruff, Kasravi, and Comp, 2010) and more diverse majors (IIE, 2011), it is becoming increasingly clear that simply offering a greater variety of study abroad programs will not broaden the demographic profile of who studies abroad or dramatically increase the number of students studying abroad. If ambitious participation goals are to be met, understanding the factors that contribute to study abroad participation is necessary.

Developing a full understanding of the factors that ultimately influence study abroad participation requires an appropriately nuanced understanding of the way in which students make decisions about educational opportunities. Without such a framework it is difficult to separate post hoc rationalizations for studying abroad from factors that legitimately influence the decision to study abroad. Moreover, without such information is it is difficult for educators to know where to exert their efforts to improve study abroad participation for those groups that have historically been underrepresented. Originally proposed to better explain the decision-making process of choosing whether enroll in postsecondary education, Paulsen and St. John's (2002) student choice construct asserts that the moment when a student actually attends class on the first day of his first semester is not preceded by a simple and singular decision. Instead, this "decision" to enter the classroom and sit down in an empty chair is preceded by a long and complex sequence of choices that perpetually reshape the likelihood of ultimately enrolling in college. Along the way, the result of each decision either expands or inhibits future opportunities for, and the likelihood of, actual matriculation. As Salisbury and his colleagues have asserted (Salisbury, Paulsen, and Pascarella, 2010, 2011; Salisbury, Umbach, Paulsen, and Pascarella, 2009), when combined with Perna's integrated model of student choice (2006), this framework presents a useful lens for understanding the factors that influence study abroad participation patterns.

Salisbury, Umbach, Paulsen, and Pascarella (2009) and Salisbury, Paulsen, and Pascarella (2010, 2011) argue that the process from initial consideration to actual departure may take months or years, beginning with various interests and capital accumulated before college. The choice to study abroad is influenced by various individual and contextual resources, such as socioeconomic status, availability of information about study abroad, previous travel abroad, perceived importance of study abroad, and language proficiency, as well as the home and school context. Generally, these factors can be organized under four broad categories: human capital (knowledge or skills that could be advantageously increased by studying abroad), economic capital (funds available to invest in study abroad), social capital (information or networks that increase one's ability to gain access to study abroad), and cultural capital (attitudes and values that contribute to increased social strata, prestige, and cultural refinement). In addition to directly influencing the decision to study abroad, factors within these categories can be mediated by structural variables such as graduation or degree requirements and institutional climate. (See Paulsen and St. John, 2002, and Perna, 2006, for an extended discussion of these various forms of capital and their relationship to educational decision making. See Salisbury, Umbach, Paulsen, and Pascarella, 2009, and Salisbury, Paulsen and Pascarella, 2011, for an extended discussion of this conceptual framework in the context of study abroad participation and intent.)

We use these types of capital to loosely organize or discuss student participation in study abroad with three caveats. First, it is often difficult to separate different forms of capital when discussing the research on influences on study abroad, as the researchers themselves often do not frame their variables as forms of capital. Second, although there is little research establishing a causal relationship between intention to study abroad and actual participation, a preliminary analysis of Wabash National data suggests that there is a very strong correlation between the two. Other researchers (for example, Heisel and Stableski, 2009) suggest there is a gap between intent and actual participation and that many students who express an interest do not follow through and take part in study abroad programs. Although the final word on this relationship awaits further study, it is clear that intention is an important variable in study abroad research. Finally, there may be a tendency to interpret the "intent" research based on the college choice model as adapted by Salisbury and colleagues to be more rational than it is and than the authors intend.

Although research in this vein attempts to predict who will study abroad, it typically recognizes that such decisions occur in contexts that interact with characteristics such as gender and race to construct the possibilities of study abroad. (See Zemach-Bersin, 2009, for an alternative view of student decisions to study abroad. Lucas, 2009, also offers an alternative conception of the decision-making process for male students.)

In the sections that follow, we first review actual participation in study abroad. We then review some factors affecting study abroad participation in general. The bulk of our review centers around the three variables considered most important in study abroad participation rates: gender, race/ethnicity, and major. Within these larger groupings we will loosely attempt to organize the research by human, financial, social, and cultural capital explanations for why students do or do not intend to study abroad. We also note that some of the research we review in this section is focused specifically on intent to study abroad, while some focuses on actual participation and some does not specify.

Who Studies Abroad

As noted earlier, students who study abroad have historically been overwhelmingly white; more female than male by a ratio of almost 2:1; of traditional college-going age; primarily majoring in the humanities, social sciences, and fine arts; and enrolled at liberal arts colleges (Commission on the Abraham Lincoln Study Abroad Fellowship Program, 2005; IIE, 2009; NAFSA, 2003; Stallman, Woodruff, Kasravi, and Comp, 2010). When talking about underrepresented populations in study abroad, then, we must include men; racial and ethnic minorities; students majoring in business, science, technology, engineering, and math (STEM) fields and students with disabilities; and community college students. It is important to note that, while the most reliable data on participation come from the annual IIE Open Doors Report, these data in and of themselves present some problems. For example, they rely on colleges and universities having and reporting accurate participation data. Second, although Open Doors reports the number of students participating in study abroad by major, gender, and race/ethnicity, it does not situate those data in the larger context of the overall number of majors in a particular field, for example.

Gender

The participation of women in study abroad has been documented consistently as twice that of men, and this statistic has changed very little over time (Dessoff, 2006; Fischer, 2012; Obst, Bhandari, and Witherell, 2007; Redden, 2008; Stallman, Woodruff, Kasravi, and Comp, 2010). In 2000–2001, women constituted 65 percent of all study abroad students; in 2009–2010 the percentage had dropped to 63.5 (IIE, n.d.b). Over the decade, then, men's participation in study abroad has increased from 35 percent to 36.5 percent of all study abroad students.

Racial/Ethnic Minorities

The historical underrepresentation of racial and ethnic minorities in higher education overall is reflected in study abroad as well. In 2009–2010, 78.7 percent of study abroad participants were white, while 21.3 percent of all students who studied abroad were racial/ethnic minorities. Some gains in racial/ethnic minority participation have been made over the decade. In 2000–2001 whites constituted 84.3 percent of all study abroad students compared to 15.7 percent for racial/ethnic minorities (IIE, n.d.b).

As a percentage of the total study abroad population in 2009–2010, racial/ethnic group participation was as follows: Asian American/Pacific Islander (7.9 percent), Hispanic/Latino(a) (6.4 percent), African American (4.7 percent), multiracial (1.9 percent), and Native American/Alaskan Native students (0.5 percent). This racial portrait of study abroad has changed minimally since 2000–2001. The percentage of Asian, Native Hawaiian/Other Pacific Islander participants of the total study abroad population increased over the decade from 5.4 percent to 7.9 percent, Hispanics from 5.4 percent to 6.4 percent, and African Americans from 3.5 percent to 4.7 percent (IIE, n.d.b). The slow pace of change in these patterns has prompted considerable investigation into the factors that might account for low levels of participation among students from traditionally underrepresented populations.

Majors

Historically speaking, study abroad has been the domain of students in the humanities and social sciences. Stallman, Woodruff, Kasravi, and Comp (2010) posit, "With curricular emphases on international, intercultural, and foreign language themes, it has been easy to encourage students in these disciplines to augment their education with time spent abroad" (p. 142). This still holds true today (Paus and Robinson, 2008; Stroud, 2010), although the preponderance of humanities and social science majors in study abroad has changed somewhat as a reflection of shifts in overall higher education enrollment (Obst, Bhandari, and Witherell, 2007; Stallman, Woodruff, Kasravi, and Comp, 2010) and increased emphasis on international experience by business schools and their national associations (Presley, Damron-Martinez, and Zhang, 2010; Relyea, Cocchiara, and Studdard, 2008).

The 2011 Open Doors report indicates that 20.7 percent of all students studying abroad in 2009–2010 were social science majors, 19.5 percent business majors, 12.1 percent humanities majors, 7.3 percent fine or applied arts, and 7.3 percent from the physical and life sciences, while only 6.1 percent were foreign language majors. The remaining majors each had 4 percent or less of the total study abroad population. The number of study abroad participants in several majors changed fairly significantly from the previous year: social science majors increased by 12 percent, business majors increased by 19.5 percent, and physics and life science majors by 6.8 percent, while foreign language majors decreased by 1.2 percent. The other major experiencing dramatic changes was engineering. Although only 3.2 percent of the total study abroad students are engineering majors, the number of engineering students studying abroad increased by 26.7 percent from 2010 (IIE, 2011).

Specifically, the growth of study abroad participants majoring in business and STEM fields and the attendant decrease in humanities majors, have contributed to a slightly different picture of study abroad by major (Stallman, Woodruff, Kasravi, and Comp, 2010). Nevertheless, majors from the humanities and social sciences remain disproportionately represented compared to business and STEM fields (Obst, Bhandari, and Witherell, 2007).

Community College Students

Community college students participate in study abroad at considerably lower rates than students from other kinds of institutions (Dessoff, 2006; Obst, Bhandari, and Witherell, 2007; Zhang, 2011). According to IIE, 5,347 community college students studied abroad in 2008–2009 (IIE, 2010), a small percentage indeed of the more than 7 million students enrolled in community colleges in 2008 (NCES, n.d.). Moreover, Salisbury, Umbach, Paulsen, and Pascarella (2009) found that students at community colleges and regional public universities are less likely to intend to participate in study abroad than those at liberal arts colleges. Given the large proportion of undergraduate students who attend U.S. community colleges, it is clear they represent a potential source of growth in the total number of students studying abroad (Goodman, 2008; Obst, Bhandari, and Witherell, 2007; Zhang, 2011). Indeed, Raby (2008) argues that community colleges that neglect to promote and support international educational experiences are delinquent in their institutional duty to adequately prepare students for the future.

Preferred Destinations

Despite expansion of study abroad beyond Europe and other English-speaking countries, European countries (United Kingdom, Italy, Spain, and France) still occupy the top four places as the most popular study abroad destinations attracting nearly 40 percent of all study abroad students in 2009–2010 (IIE, 2011). China is now fourth, with 5.1 percent of the total. In fact, of the top twenty-five destinations, eleven are European and seven Spanish-speaking Americas, with Australia, Japan, South Africa, India, Israel, and New Zealand rounding out the top twenty-five. While the top fifteen destinations remain largely unchanged since 1999–2000, South Africa (1.6 percent) and India (1.4 percent) are the notable newcomers to the list, at numbers thirteen and fourteen, with 1.6 percent and 1.4 percent of the total study abroad population, respectively, in 2009–2010. Conversely, the United Kingdom's share of the total has decreased from 20 percent to 12.1 percent.

Factors Affecting Intent to Study Abroad and Participation Rates

Several general factors affect intent and actual participation in study abroad. Much of the focus is on barriers to participation.

Socioeconomic Status

Socioeconomic status and parental income are among the primary factors influencing the decision to study abroad (Salisbury, Umbach, Paulsen, and Pascarella, 2009). Socioeconomic status is positively related to intent to study abroad; lower-income students are less likely than higher-income students to intend to study abroad. Parental level of education is also related to intentions to study abroad. Salisbury, Umbach, Paulsen, and Pascarella (2009) conclude that taken together socioeconomic status and parental income constitute a powerful influence on whether a student considers study abroad. The Wesleyan University (an elite, private university) students interviewed by Zemach-Bersin (2009) thought of study abroad as a normal part of the college experience. They expected to do it. Lower-income students likely do not have the same expectations.

Lack of Information

Much of the literature cites lack of awareness of study abroad programs as a limitation to participation for all students (Brown, 2002; Brux and Fry, 2010; Dessoff, 2006; Perdreau, 2003; Salisbury, Umbach, Paulsen, and Pascarella, 2009; Sommer, 2003; Stallman, Woodruff, Kasravi, and Comp, 2010; Van Der Meid, 2003). Unawareness about study abroad opportunities may be attributed to an inability to find appropriate information. This may stem from ineffective marketing, few peer role models, or simply not knowing where to look. Students may not be the only ones who lack awareness of study abroad. Brown (2002) and Dessoff (2006) allude to ignorance of potential study abroad opportunities on the part of institutional leaders, such as faculty members and advisors, as well. Misinformation or myths may also discourage students from studying abroad. For example, Hamir (2011) found that students believed that studying abroad would delay graduation despite evidence to the contrary. An additional aspect of information in the decision-making process is where and from whom students get information or encouragement to study abroad. In the qualitative component of her study, Hamir found that friends and family were high on the positive end, whereas faculty members were disturbingly low. Gore (2005) argues that the advertising messages may unintentionally promote the view that study abroad is for women.

Involvement

Other indicators of social and cultural capital affect predisposition to study abroad positively. These include high interest in reading and writing, openness to diversity, attending a liberal arts college, and majoring in the social sciences. Campus practices enhancing diverse interactions and cocurricular involvement were significantly and positively related to intentions to study abroad (Salisbury, Umbach, Paulsen, and Pascarella, 2009). Interestingly, involvement in high school activities seems to have a small but negative effect overall (Salisbury, Umbach, Paulsen, and Pascarella, 2009). Exploring how student involvement affects plans to study abroad, Rust, Dhanatya, Furuto, and Kheiltash (2007) devised five scales gauging different types of involvement. The most predictive scale was that of diversity, suggesting that students who frequently interact socially with members of other racial/ethnic groups and who are interested in improving cross-cultural and racial understanding are significantly more likely to plan to go abroad than those who are involved in other ways. Following diversity involvement, the predictive ability of the other scales in respective order were social, political, community, and academic, indicating that activities such as social interaction with peers, political interest and activity, and volunteerism influence students' plans to study abroad. Salisbury, Umbach, Paulsen, and Pascarella (2009) also found that diverse experiences during the first year of college could improve the likelihood of intent to study abroad, suggesting that systemic attitudinal differences between students who intend and students who do not intend to study abroad may not be entirely solidified prior to matriculation. Salisbury, Umbach, Paulsen, and Pascarella (2009) found that involvement affected men's and women's intent to study abroad differently. We discuss this further below.

Attitudes

It is not only having diverse experiences that fosters interest in study abroad. A small subset of findings suggests that study abroad participants may differ from those who do not participate in their attitudes toward intercultural interaction, their interest in intercultural experiences, and the degree to which they value intercultural interaction as a part of their college education. Stroud (2010) found that students who expressed an interest in improving their understanding of other cultures and countries were twice as likely to intend to study abroad as those who did not.

Kim and Goldstein (2005) and Goldstein and Kim (2006) looked at measures of intercultural attitude as predictive of favorable expectations toward study abroad. In both studies, intercultural attitude was defined by variables such as prejudice, ethnocentrism, intolerance of ambiguity, apprehension about intercultural communication, and language interest and competence. Perhaps not surprisingly, the authors found support for their hypotheses that low levels of ethnocentrism and high levels of language interest predicted favorable expectations of study abroad. Students with higher levels of ethnocentrism and prejudice were less likely to study abroad; females demonstrated lower levels of ethnocentrism and higher levels of interest in foreign language (Goldstein and Kim, 2006). Language competence and tolerance of ambiguity were not predictive in either study. Kim and Goldstein initially found that low levels of intercultural communication apprehension were indicative of interest in study abroad, but over the long term this was not found to be significant (Goldstein and Kim, 2006). Interestingly, Goldstein and Kim (2006) discovered that "expectations and intercultural variables played a far more critical role in determining who studied abroad than academic or career factors" (p. 517) a finding supported by Rust, Dhanatya, Furuto, and Kheiltash (2007).

As a part of the Study Abroad Evaluation Project, Carlson, Burn, Useem, and Yachimovicz (1990) asked both the study abroad students and the control group (that is, students who remained on campus) a series of questions about international knowledge and interest and intercultural aptitudes at the beginning of their study prior to departure. The researchers identified clear differences in the degree to which the two groups of students viewed American foreign policy (the study abroad students were more critical of American foreign policy), the quality of postsecondary education in Western European countries (the study abroad students held more positive opinions), and degree of interest in experiencing other cultures (the study abroad students were much more interested in experiencing other cultures than the students who were not about to study abroad).

Motivations

Students' motivations for studying abroad are undoubtedly related to various sources of human, economic, social, and cultural capital. Students go abroad for a variety of reasons. One long-standing motive for study abroad is to improve one's foreign language skills, the belief being that time spent immersed in the target culture will facilitate improved linguistic ability (Allen, 2010). Goldstein and Kim (2006) replicated earlier findings of King and Young (1994) that students who studied abroad tended to be more interested in learning a foreign language. Interest in foreign languages may be suggestive of curiosity about and respect for other cultures.

In a related manner, then, some students may choose to go abroad in hopes of cultural gain (Goldstein and Kim, 2006). In the case of heritage seekers, for instance, the intention is to integrate oneself into the host culture as much as possible given programmatic time constraints (Comp, 2008; Tsantir and Titus, 2006). We discuss heritage seekers in greater detail in the section on racial/ethnic minority participation. Others may simply be interested in diversity or cultural understanding. Salisbury, Umbach, Paulsen, and Pascarella (2009) and Stroud (2010) both found that the degree to which students value developing cross-cultural understanding during college significantly increased the likelihood of intending to study abroad.

Another common rationale for participating in study abroad is career related. That is, many students want to go overseas while in school in order to improve their future job prospects (Dessoff, 2006; Relyea, Cocchiara, and Studdard, 2008). McKeown (2003) attributed an upsurge in study abroad interest post-9/11 to the fact that more students now seem to consider study abroad an important academic and professional experience. Moreover, the students in McKeown's study appear to pay more heed to the notion that learning another language is imperative.

Finally, but certainly not least, is studying abroad for pleasure. Some students may envision study abroad as a break from the rigors of undergraduate education, a kind of overseas tour for academic credit (He and Chen, 2010; Zemach-Bersin, 2009) or for adventure (Lucas, 2009; Zemach-Bersin, 2009). He and Chen (2010) found that two of the most important factors in student decisions to study abroad were related to tourism and social contact. Language study, quality of education, and course content were middling influences; religion was the least influential.

While these personal motivations expose a range of impetuses to study abroad, that is not to say they are mutually exclusive. More likely, it is a combination of all of the above that impels any one student to participate in study abroad (Allen, 2010; Lucas, 2009; Rust, Dhanatya, Furuto, and Kheiltash, 2007). Indeed, entirely different goals often coexist within the same program and within an individual student (Allen, 2010). In combination, these studies indicate that the individual motives for a student to decide whether to participate in study abroad can be multiple and concurrent. They interact in complex ways with students' human, economic, social, and cultural capital to produce an interest in study abroad. We now consider in more depth research pertaining to intent to study abroad participation for several groups traditionally underrepresented in study abroad.

Factors Affecting Men's and Women's Participation

Although the percentages have shifted ever so slightly, women continue to represent the majority of study abroad students, and their interest in studying abroad remains higher than that of men. In their 2009 study of intent to study abroad using data from the Wabash National Study of the Liberal Arts, Salisbury, Umbach, Paulsen and Pascarella (2009) found that men were 8 percent less likely than women to intend to study abroad, confirming previous research (for example, Dessoff, 2006). There are numerous possible explanations for why more women than men study abroad, though Redden (2008) claims that a dearth of theoretical research on the topic has made it impossible to thoroughly account for the discrepant rates. Women's participation rates are particularly notable in light of several qualitative studies documenting that women face additional challenges in the study abroad setting that men do not (Anderson, 2003; Polanyi, 1995; Talburt and Stewart, 1999; Twombly, 1995). Generally the reasons provided for women's higher rates of participation are educated guesses rooted in history and observation (Redden, 2008; Salisbury, Paulsen, and Pascarella, 2010).

In the most extensive study to examine the gender gap in study abroad intent, Salisbury, Paulsen, and Pascarella (2010), using data from the Wabash National Study of Liberal Arts, concluded that "gendered differences play an important and varied role in shaping the ways that men and women develop interests in participating in study abroad programs during college" (p. 632). We highlight several of the key findings from that study here:

- Race and ethnicity interact with gender to produce differential interests in studying abroad. For example, Asian American men were less likely to intend to study abroad than Asian American women. In addition, Hispanic women are more likely than white women to intend to study abroad but Hispanic men's intentions did not differ from those of white men.
- The authors found no statistically significant differences between men and women on variables typically considered to represent human or economic capital. They did, however, find several differences between men and women on various measures of social and cultural capital both before and during college. Regarding social capital, while higher levels of parental education increased intent to study abroad among women, parental education had no effect on men's study abroad intent. Likewise, involvement in high school negatively affected men's intent to study abroad but had no effect on women. Regarding cultural capital, while openness to diversity affected both men and women positively with respect to study abroad plans, an increase in openness to diversity among men produced a significantly larger increase in the likelihood of study abroad intent than a similar increase produced in women.
- Women who attended community colleges or regional institutions were less likely than women attending liberal arts colleges to intend to study abroad while institutional context had no impact on male study abroad intent. Two curricular experiences seemed to impact male and female study abroad

intent differently. An increase in scores on an integrative learning experiences scale increased men's intent to study abroad, while it decreased intent for women. In addition, an increase in the number of diversity courses taken had a positive effect on women's intentions but none on men. Outside of class, an increase in peer interactions both in high school and in college had no effect on women's intentions but negatively shaped men's study abroad intent.

Major

Dessoff (2006), Stallman, Woodruff, Kasravi, and Comp (2010), and Thomas and McMahon (1998), among others, posit that higher participation rates by women may be attributed to the fields of study that women choose to pursue. Foreign language majors, for instance, have typically been logical candidates for study abroad based on the assumption that immersion is requisite for linguistic fluency. Accordingly, Kim and Goldstein (2005) and Goldstein and Kim (2006) found that language interest was significantly higher in female students than male students. Other areas of study well represented among study abroad students, including the social sciences, humanities, and fine arts, also show a preponderance of female enrollment (Turner and Bowen, 1999). While rates of study abroad participation by women coincide with their representation in certain majors to some extent, this fact does not sufficiently explain why rates remain higher even for women in male-dominated fields such as business and engineering (Redden, 2008).

In fact, Salisbury, Paulsen, and Pascarella (2010) found few unique effects of major on men's and women's intent to study abroad. Similar percentages of men and women were undecided in their choice of major, but only undecided men were more likely than men intending to major in humanities, fine arts, or foreign languages to intend to study abroad. Being undecided did not have a significant effect on women's intent to study abroad.

Higher female participation rates have also been attributed to overall rates of female participation in higher education (Redden, 2008; Stallman, Woodruff, Kasravi, and Comp, 2010). This explanation is weakened by the fact that women only recently have come to constitute a majority of undergraduate students, while women's overrepresentation among study abroad participants has long been noted.

These quantitative accounts for unequal participation rates have been balanced with attempts to further explore the disproportion of women in study abroad from a more qualitative perspective. Redden (2008) cites research done by Jill McKinney, associate director of the Center for Global Education at Butler University, who found three reasons to explain why women participate more readily than men—age, motherhood, and safety. She concludes that women who want to have children may view study abroad as a unique and timely opportunity to travel overseas, one that they may not necessarily have again in the future. Women may also feel safer traveling in groups, or it may be viewed as more socially and culturally appropriate for them to travel overseas as part of a structured program with other students (Bowman, 1987).

Reasons for Lower Male Participation

Conversely, although they do not provide a detailed explanation as to why this may be, Stallman, Woodruff, Kasravi, and Comp (2010) conjecture that "[t]he lower percentage of males studying abroad may be connected to family and other external obligations in the U.S., the lack of flexibility within academic field of study, and the perception of study abroad as a female domain" (p. 147). Salisbury, Umbach, Paulsen, and Pascarella (2009) posit a couple of interesting hypotheses for men's lower rates of participation. First, they note that diversity experiences seem to have a greater effect on men's interest in study abroad than they do on women (although such experiences positively influence both). Involvement in college, however, appears to have a negative effect on men's intent to study abroad. When looking at the negative effects of high school involvement and the negative effects of increased peer interactions during the first year of college on men's intent to participate, one can only surmise that there is something about the social interactions before and in the first year of college that discourages men from thinking about study abroad. It is also clear that integrative learning experiences are important for men.

Taking a holistic approach, Lucas (2009) uses the classification of college students as idlers, players, workers or strategists to help him understand male motivations for studying abroad or not. Most of the students interviewed fit the player or worker category. Players do not want a study abroad experience that is too structured or too planned while workers react negatively to messages that study abroad is about having fun or adventure. In short, Lucas argues that the marketing messages promoting study abroad communicate a feminized vision of study abroad that misses what men value and want to get out of it. For men, the benefits should outweigh the opportunity costs of being away from friends and school. These benefits are not portrayed in study abroad literature.

In sum, the research suggests that factors contributing to students' intentions to study abroad are not the same for men and women. Given the observed high proportion of women who participate in study abroad and the lower numbers of men who envision study abroad as part of their undergraduate experience, it is clear that further studies in this area are needed.

Factors Affecting Study Abroad Participation for Racial and Ethnic Minorities

Racial and ethnic minority participation in study abroad represents a complex interaction among various factors, including gender and major. Salisbury, Umbach, Paulsen, and Pascarella (2009) found that Asian Pacific Islanders were 15 percentage points less likely than whites to express intent to study abroad. They also found that other racial/ethnic groups did not differ from whites in intent to study abroad. Thus, they conclude that it is not for lack of interest that members of racial and ethnic minorities groups participate at lower rates than whites.

Individual and Human Capital

Several individual or human capital factors have been identified in the existing research that contribute to racial/ethnic minority student interest in or actual participation in study abroad. Salisbury, Paulsen, and Pascarella (2011) found that an increase in ACT/SAT actually decreased the likelihood that African Americans intended to study abroad. A second individual variable is gender. As noted earlier, males across all racial groups, minority as well as white, are less likely to intend to study abroad than their female counterparts (Rust, Dhanatya, Furuto, and Kheiltash, 2008). This observation is especially salient when it comes to those males who identify as Asian American or Pacific

Islander (Salisbury, Paulsen, and Pascarella, 2010; Salisbury, Paulsen, and Pascarella, 2011). Van Der Meid (2003) compared groups of Asian American students who had participated in study abroad to those who had not and found that Asian American females in the study abroad group outnumbered males by a ratio of 5 to 1.

Gender, however, is only one potential factor. For students from under-represented racial and ethnic groups who have the desire to take advantage of study abroad, a host of other issues may effectively discourage them from considering studying abroad and from not participating (Brux and Fry, 2010; Dessoff, 2006; Salisbury, Paulsen, and Pascarella, 2011; Stallman, Woodruff, Kasravi, and Comp, 2010). Among others, these constraints consist of institutional barriers, cultural differences, nonacademic responsibilities, fears about safety and discrimination, and, most prominently, financial concerns.

Financial

Financial concerns are particularly prominent among the reasons cited for low minority student participation in study abroad, although the effect they have on participation varies by racial/ethnic group (Brown, 2002; Brux and Fry, 2010; Dessoff, 2006; Penn and Tanner, 2009; Stallman, Woodruff, Kasravi, and Comp, 2010; Van Der Meid, 2003). Salisbury, Paulsen, and Pascarella (2011) reinforced the importance of financial capital on decisions to study abroad. Salisbury, Umbach, Paulsen, and Pascarella (2009) and Salisbury, Paulsen, and Pascarella (2011) found that types and sources of financial aid affected racial groups' intent to study abroad differently. Hispanic students who receive federal grants are more likely to study abroad than those who do not, but the same is not true for white students. However, receiving a loan, which seems to have no effect on white students, appears to be a deterrent to study abroad for Hispanic students. For Asian American students, institutional grants significantly affect positive intent to study abroad. As Salisbury, Paulsen, and Pascarella (2011) note, "[a]lthough student loans may assist in increasing access to higher education, it may only be through grants that additional financial aid can positively influence study abroad participation" (p. 145). This finding is reinforced by other scholars as well (Brown, 2002; Perdreau, 2003; Stallman, Woodruff, Kasravi, and Comp, 2010). Apparently, then, even when financial assistance to support study abroad exists, students of different ethnic/racial groups view types of assistance differently in their decision making. Salisbury, Paulsen, and Pascarella's (2011) findings suggest that institutional and federal financial aid in the form of grants may hold potential for increasing racial and ethnic minority students' rates of participation in study abroad. In the past, it seems that fewer students were conscious of the possibility to apply federal financial funds to overseas education (Stallman, Woodruff, Kasravi, and Comp, 2010); now, it is becoming more common practice to apply financial aid funds to education abroad, provided the programs that students take part in confer institutionally accepted credit. As such, researchers argue that study abroad administrators should work in tandem with institutions' financial aid departments in order to put study abroad within reach of students who would otherwise consider it an impossibility (Burr, 2005; Perdreau, 2003; Pickard and Ganz, 2005).

Interestingly, Van Der Meid (2003) suggests that financial concerns may be more of a perceived rather than actual constraint to studying abroad. In his study, students who had no study abroad experience were concerned about the potential cost of studying abroad whereas those who had gone abroad and returned were much less concerned about cost. This suggests two explanations: racial/ethnic minority students simply misperceive the real costs of study abroad, a finding supported by Penn and Tanner (2009), or it may confirm findings that those who study abroad are financially able to do so and would be less concerned about cost.

Simply offering financial aid, however, may not be enough to increase participation of racial and ethnic minority students (Perdreau, 2003). Research into racial/ethnic minority students' intentions and participation suggests another significant deterrent: that study abroad is not traditionally viewed as a necessary or worthwhile academic pursuit (Brown, 2002; Brux and Fry, 2010; Calhoon, Wildcat, and Annett, 2003; Perdreau, 2003; Salisbury, Paulsen, and Pascarella, 2011).

Perceptions of Who Should Study Abroad

The view that study abroad is frivolous, irrelevant, or simply not for them may be especially significant for first-generation college students, many of whom are from racial/ethnic minority groups (Burr, 2005; Dessoff, 2006). According to Burr (2005) Hispanic students thought that study abroad was primarily for high-income students.

Lack of Role Models

In conjunction with cultural influences and family support, researchers have suggested that the lack of fictional and real role models contributes to this belief that study abroad is not useful or appropriate (Brux and Fry, 2010; Jackson, 2005; Penn and Tanner, 2009; Perdreau, 2003). Moreover, films may portray study abroad as the province of young, white women (Jackson, 2005). Additionally, minority students who have studied abroad in the past may not share information about their experiences with potential future participants (Brown, 2002; Brux and Fry, 2010; Jackson, 2005; Perdreau, 2003). The ultimate effect of having few visible examples available to minority students may be that they "don't think of study abroad as right for them and they then filter out or ignore information about study abroad" (Brux and Fry, 2010, p. 515).

Institutional Barriers

Institutionally created barriers, some of which correspond to aspects of social and cultural capital identified by Salisbury, Paulsen, and Pascarella (2011), affect participation in study abroad across all student groups, but they can be particularly challenging for racial/ethnic minority students. Examples of institutional types of barriers include lack of information, limited faculty support, inappropriate or ineffective marketing, and curricular constraints (Brown, 2002; Brux and Fry, 2010; Stallman, Woodruff, Kasravi, and Comp, 2010; Van Der Meid, 2003). In addition, scarcity of institutional support and resources may affect a minority-serving institution's ability to offer study abroad programs to its students (Calhoon, Wildcat, and Annett, 2003).

Although insufficient awareness or lack of information is often mentioned as a cause for low levels of minority student study abroad participation, some researchers have found that it is not a genuine deterrent. For example, the students in Brux and Fry's (2010) study were aware of study abroad programs offered by the university, were keen to go abroad, and were supported by certain faculty and staff. Rather, the biggest constraining factor for these students was financial, followed by issues with academic scheduling, nonacademic responsibilities such as work and family, ill-fitting program offerings, and fears for safety. Similarly, the Asian Americans who chose not to study abroad in Van Der Meid's (2003) study indicated complete awareness of the study abroad opportunities available to them. Issues of academic compatibility and financial concerns were more relevant to their decisions.

Major and Program Fit

A seemingly significant institutional barrier to racial/ethnicity minority student participation in study abroad appears to be related to academic major and program fit. African Americans, in particular, are underrepresented in some of the majors with highest study abroad participation rates (Penn and Tanner, 2009). Consideration of how time invested in study abroad can be tailored to fit with students' broader undergraduate careers is salient across all student groups, including students from racial and ethnic minority groups. Both Brux and Fry (2010) and Van Der Meid (2003) acknowledge that worries about whether study abroad is appropriate in terms of time and major can serve as disincentives to participate. Interestingly, however, when Salisbury, Paulsen, and Pascarella (2011) looked specifically at racial/ethnic groups, they found that higher degree aspirations by African Americans and Asian Americans effectively increased interest in study abroad whereas they substantially decreased interest in study abroad for white students.

Also pertinent to underrepresented students is the relevancy of program locations and topics. A lack of programs of interest curbs intent to study abroad (Brux and Fry, 2010; Calhoon, Wildcat, and Annett, 2003; Comp, 2008; Van Der Meid, 2003). Calhoon, Wildcat, and Annett (2003) suggest that study abroad for Native American students should be related to culturally respected interests like community and ecology. Brux and Fry (2010) found that the African American and Asian American students clearly indicated interest in studying abroad in places associated with their ancestry. In addition, they indicated preference for program topics related to their heritage. This finding is somewhat at odds with Penn and Tanner's finding that Europe was a favored destination for pre-college African American high school students. A case study undertaken by Tsantir and Titus (2006) suggested that the experiences of students of color who engage in study abroad based on their ethnic origins are different than those of their white counterparts. According to Tsantir and Titus (2006), students base decisions on where to study abroad more on heritage than on major.

Heritage Seeking

A small body of research exists about choosing a study abroad destination based on one's ancestry or racial/ethnic background, or what is often called heritage seeking (Jorge, 2006; Szekely, 1998, as cited in Comp, 2008). According to Rubin (2004), students who engage in heritage seeking at present do so in order to facilitate better communication with family members at home and to establish their own opinions about the land of their family's cultural roots. Parental support, however, is not a given nor is seamless inclusion in the host culture (Comp, 2008; Rubin, 2004; Tsantir and Titus, 2006). Although heritage-seeking is not necessarily a new phenomenon as it relates to study abroad, it does present an opportunity for those institutions that are interested in bolstering minority student participation in study abroad to create programs more focused on the interests of students of color in a broader range of locations (Brown, 2002; Brux and Fry, 2010; Rubin, 2004; Stallman, Woodruff, Kasravi, and Comp, 2010; Tsantir and Titus, 2006; Zachrisson, 2005).

Family Support

Related to heritage seeking is the issue of cultural acceptance and community support for study abroad. The students in Burr's (2005) study indicated that they would not necessarily be able to garner any familial support, financial or otherwise, even if they wanted to go abroad. Through interviews with the students' parents, the author discovered that strict guidelines would need to be followed if the parents were to allow their children to participate in study abroad, including the need to travel in a group with classmates and a faculty member. McClure, Niehaus, Anderson, and Reed (2010) found that, despite positive perceptions of the potential educational value of study abroad among a small sample of Hispanic students, family connections and obligations, financial issues, and a lack of access to information about study abroad opportunities played a role in making study abroad seem just out of reach. Tsantir and

Titus's (2006) case study of heritage seekers found that parental support greatly influenced students' choice of study abroad program. Furthermore, students are strongly influenced by their peers and their family when it comes to making decisions about whether to study abroad (Brown, 2002; Brux and Fry, 2010; Burr, 2005; Perdreau, 2003; Tsantir and Titus, 2006; Van Der Meid, 2003). More broadly, it may be that the respective cultures of some minority students impede interest in or acceptance of study abroad as a valid educational undertaking.

Whereas Burr (2005) revealed potential familial support for first-generation Hispanic students interested in going abroad, Salisbury, Paulsen, and Pascarella (2011) found the opposite for Asian Americans. That is, the authors found that decreased interest in participation by Asian Americans could be attributed, in part, to higher levels of parental education, "reflecting a more narrow view of the postsecondary experiences necessary to prepare college graduates for a successful personal and professional life" (p. 143). Comparing Asian American students who studied abroad with those who did not, Van Der Meid (2003) found that the highest percentage of those to go abroad were U.S.-born, second-generation Asian Americans. For those who chose not to study abroad, he found that "a shorter amount of time residing in the United States decreases the chance that a student will study abroad" (p. 102). In other words, low levels of Asian American participation in study abroad are partly attributable to the fact that newer Asian immigrant groups may retain their cultural origins and may not yet have adopted study abroad as an American educational cultural norm (Brux and Fry, 2010; Van Der Meid, 2003).

Fears of Discrimination

Being subject to discrimination in their domestic daily lives, minority students may not participate in study abroad for fear of discrimination and concerns about safety (Brux and Fry, 2010; Perdreau, 2003; Stallman, Woodruff, Kasravi, and Comp, 2010; Van Der Meid, 2003). Such apprehension may originate with the student or the student's parents (Brux and Fry, 2010; Rubin, 2004). Comp (2008) suggests that even heritage-seeking students may have trouble being accepted into the host culture regardless of their shared physical attributes and that they may be considered "simply Americans" (p. 31).

For the Asian Americans in Van Der Meid's (2003) study, fear ranked at the bottom of deterrents to study abroad program; however, those who did study abroad acknowledged discriminatory experiences while overseas. Yet another reason given for low minority participation rates is that "they already interact across cultural differences everyday" (Salisbury, Woodruff, Kasravi, and Comp, 2011, p. 143). Calhoon, Wildcat, and Annett (2003) argue that American Indian students may refrain from participating in study abroad, particularly in Europe, because of its association with the roots of colonization and the ways in which that is interpreted within American Indian culture.

If there is a take-home message from our review of factors contributing to racial and ethnic minority student decisions to participate in study abroad, it is that the process is a complex one involving many factors. If access to study abroad is to expand and participation to be encouraged, these are some of the areas that will need to be addressed. The result would be participation rates that more accurately reflect enrollment patterns in American higher education overall.

Effects of Degree Aspirations and Field of Study on Study Abroad Participation

Perhaps because of the historic dominance of foreign language and social science majors among study abroad participants, there has been little attention to barriers to study abroad for other majors until recently. Efforts to increase global competencies in all students have resulted in considerable attention to how to increase participation in study abroad across all majors. Some of the obstacles related to participation are related to the time it takes for students to complete their declared degree, levels of institutional and faculty support, and disciplinary structure. These hurdles to study abroad participation appear to manifest themselves differently according to degree aspirations and academic major.

Degree Aspirations

Generally, it seems that students with higher degree aspirations tend to shy away from taking part in study abroad (Stroud, 2010) although Salisbury,

Paulsen, and Pascarella (2011) found that this only held true for white students. For African Americans and Asian Americans, the interaction of race and plans to pursue a graduate degree had the opposite effect. That is, they expressed desire to study abroad as well as intent to continue their postbaccalaureate education. There is a gap, however, between intent to study abroad and actually doing so. When Salisbury, Umbach, Paulsen, and Pascarella (2009) investigated intentions to study abroad in higher education, major itself did not have a specific effect on intent to study abroad. Overall social science majors were more likely to express intent to study abroad. Only identification as an undecided major seemed to affect significantly students' intentions to study abroad, and it did so positively. The authors found no statistical difference in intent to study abroad between students who were majoring in humanities, business, education, or STEM fields. Similarly, Goldstein and Kim (2006) determined that neither study abroad participants nor nonparticipants demonstrated any difference according to major, time to degree, or potential future employment. In other words, there must be other nonacademic, non-job-related factors that determine whether students participate in study abroad. To some degree, what those factors are may depend on what subject students choose to pursue.

Business Majors

A considerable amount of attention has been paid to study abroad among business majors, what motivates them to study abroad (or keeps them from doing so), and what kinds of experiences they seek when they do study abroad. One of the general findings from this research is that business students engage in a form of cost-benefit analysis to assess costs and benefits to their future careers, time to degree and employability (Schnusenberg, de Jong, and Goel, 2012; Presley, Damron-Martinez, and Zhang 2010; Toncar, Reid, and Anderson, 2005). Relyea, Cocchiara, and Studdard (2008) examined the moderating effect of perceived value on business students' levels of risk propensity and their decisions to participate in study abroad. Their findings supported their hypotheses that "students who may have a high risk propensity, but see little if any value in their career outcome, will simply not want to exert the effort to participate in an international experience" (p. 356). Nevertheless, both business and nonbusiness majors had similar preferences when it came to program content, length, and destinations. Cardon, Marshall, and Poddar (2011) examined business students' preferences for certain types of study abroad programs. These business students were mainly found to prefer English-speaking and/or Western European destinations (Cardon, Marshall, and Poddar, 2011). They attributed this to the fact that nearly 79 percent of the students in their study were what they called "controlled exposure seekers" and "spontaneous dissimilarity seekers." The former "seek the least social contact but also seek cultures dissimilar to their own" whereas the latter seek "more social contact with dissimilar cultures" (p. 15). The two leading groups share a desire for recognizable, well-developed tourist infrastructure such as international hotel chains and common systems of transportation. Where these groups diverge is in the necessity for cultural similarity, level of social contact with the host country peoples, and amount of pre-trip planning.

Seeking to understand why U.S. business major participation in study abroad continues to be lower than in other countries, Sánchez, Fornerino, and Zhang (2006) compared U.S. to French and Chinese business majors. They found common motivations and barriers across U.S., Chinese, and French cultures and discovered that intent to study abroad was strongest among Chinese students. For Chinese students, study abroad was viewed as a method of enhancing future career opportunities that ideally would result in improved wealth, social status, and lifestyle. For American students the authors found that interest in study abroad was primarily driven by perceptions of it as a gateway to fun and adventure, which seems to be at odds with research suggesting business students will study abroad if the benefits outweigh the costs. Sánchez, Fornerino, and Zhang (2006) suggest that both American and French students may be less motivated to engage in an international educational experiences because "they have adequate opportunities to improve their social and professional status without studying abroad" (p. 48), whereas for Chinese students, going abroad is seen as a stepping stone to future success.

Regardless of the theory that is used to investigate business majors' intent to participate in study abroad, it is evident that the decision to go overseas for these students involves weighing institutional barriers such as time to degree against prospective occupational payoffs. As Relyea, Cocchiara, and Studdard (2008) conclude: "Students who understand that globalization has become the landscape of the business marketplace may place a higher emphasis on the value of engaging in an international experience" (p. 356). Ultimately, though, it is a question of how an individual student's decision to study abroad fits within the program constraints of the business major.

STEM

This issue of understanding impediments to study abroad is particularly salient for majors in the STEM fields. In their study, Salisbury, Umbach, Paulsen, and Pascarella (2009) noted no statistical difference between humanities, business, education, or STEM majors in terms of interest in study abroad. Even so, the percentages of study abroad students majoring in the natural sciences, technology, engineering, and math fields, although slightly higher than in the past, are undeniably lower than other majors (Obst, Bhandari, and Witherell, 2007; Paus and Robinson, 2008; Stallman, Woodruff, Kasravi, and Comp, 2010; Stroud, 2010). The most often cited reasons for this are lack of curricular flexibility and lack of faculty support. This hypothesis receives some support from Niehaus's (2011) recent research using data from the National Survey of Living Learning Programs. Her research suggests that gender and class standing are predictors of intent to study abroad. Sophomores are less likely to intend to across all majors but the drop-off appears to be greater for physical and biological science majors. Some of the drop-off may be due to interaction effects of gender as men's intent to study abroad also decreases more than women's.

Some of the reasons for this drop are provided in an unpublished qualitative evaluation of a National Science Foundation (NSF)–sponsored program supporting a multiyear study and research abroad experience for physics and engineering students in Switzerland (Twombly, 2010). The hierarchical nature of the sciences (that higher-level content depends on prerequisite learning) was a concern to both students and faculty members affecting students' unwillingness to actually enroll in, and faculty members' willingness to recommend, study abroad for credit. This concern expressed itself mainly as one of the students finding themselves behind if they could not take the right courses abroad and fears of being unprepared to take higher-level courses necessary for their major. A related concern was lack of sufficient language skills to take high-level science courses abroad. Additionally, the not-for-credit lab experience working with world-class scientists, not for-credit courses, was viewed as the most valuable résumé builder for these budding physicists.

According to O'Hara (2009), "[f]aculty in the STEM fields are even less likely than their colleagues in other fields to incorporate international perspectives into their courses" (p. 45). Nevertheless, curricular integration is precisely promoted as a method to expand institutional capacity for study abroad (Brewer and Cunningham, 2009; Gutierrez, Auerbach, and Bhandari, 2009). It appears that many institutions are making concerted efforts to increase study abroad options for STEM majors. Some examples include the University of Rhode Island's five-year engineering program option in which study abroad is a built-in component (Dessoff, 2006) and Emory University's Emory College Science Experience Abroad (SEA), in which students in subjects such as biology or chemistry can fulfill degree requirements overseas (Obst, Bhandari, and Witherell, 2007). More research on factors contributing to STEM majors' decisions to participate or not in study abroad will likely be forthcoming. Assuming curricular challenges can be addressed, STEM majors would likely be ripe for study abroad given the high percentage of international faculty members teaching in STEM disciplines in U.S. colleges and universities (Kim, Twombly, and Wolf-Wendel, 2011) and the international nature of scientific work.

Community College Students

Factors affecting study abroad positively or negatively for community college students are often attributed to personal and professional responsibilities (Dessoff, 2006; Raby, 2008; Zhang, 2011) as well as cost and institutional limitations (Falcetta, n.d.; Raby, 2008; Stallman, Woodruff, Kasravi, and Comp, 2010; Zhang, 2011). While the expense of study abroad in terms of both price and opportunity cost is certainly an essential consideration as it relates to all undergraduates, cost is likely an especially salient consideration for community college students. For the traditional community college student (the nontraditional undergraduate), however, combining study abroad with work and family may pose significant challenges for considering, much less engaging in, study abroad. Also unstated in the research is that community college students may not study abroad because they plan to transfer and could do so after transferring.

Institutional support for study abroad may also be lacking in community colleges. That is, as an entity that is strongly attached to its local roots, the promotion and encouragement of overseas learning experiences may be considered to be outside the scope of the community college mission (Raby, 2008; Zhang, 2011). As a result, it may be that infrastructure for study abroad suffers. Without funding to maintain offices of study abroad and their personnel, the ability to reach potential students and support them while they are away is severely limited (Dessoff, 2006; Raby, 2008; Stallman, Woodruff, Kasravi, and Comp, 2010; Zhang, 2011). In addition, Raby (2008) suggests that there needs to be a better understanding at the administrative level of how to make study abroad a sustainable arm of the institution.

Summary

The story of who participates in study abroad (and who does not) is pretty clear, having changed only slightly over the course of the past fifty years at least. The study abroad population is predominantly white, female, social science majors of higher socioeconomic status from liberal arts colleges. As a major academic decision point, the choice to study abroad can be understood from Paulsen and St. John's student-choice process as consisting of several stages from predisposition, through search and decision. This process occurs in a particular college context but is shaped by individual, home, and school environments such as socioeconomic factors and experiences in college.

Although the choice to go abroad occurs on an individual level, it is not made in a vacuum. "Establishing the valence of study abroad programs entails careful consideration of their perceived benefits by prospective students" (Relyea, Cocchiara, and Studdard, 2008). Prospective students' decisions to participate are ultimately based on the interaction of a number of different considerations, individual and shared (Salisbury, Umbach, Paulsen, and Pascarella, 2009; Salisbury, Paulsen, and Pascarella, 2010; Salisbury Paulsen, and Pascarella, 2011). The influence of family and peers is strong (Paus and Robinson, 2008), and society in general may hold some sway insofar as the need for study abroad as a means of addressing globalization is reflected in national policy, but the role of the institution should not be underestimated. In fact, some would argue that the institution's role is fundamental (Pearson, 2005; Salisbury, Umbach, Paulsen, and Pascarella, 2009; Whalen, 2009). Certainly, to reach the ambitious goals set for study abroad participation, institutions must find additional ways to increase awareness, interest, and participation in study abroad.

Study Abroad Outcomes[5]

A MERICAN EDUCATIONAL POLICYMAKERS, employers, and higher education leaders have recognized that American college graduates must acquire the ability to communicate and collaborate across racial, ethnic, and cultural differences if they are to successfully engage, compete, and contribute in "the new global century" (AAC&U, 2007; APLU, 2004; Bikson, Treverton, Moini, and Lindstrom, 2003; Commission on the Abraham Lincoln Study Abroad Fellowship Program, 2005). To this end, postsecondary institutions and organizations have invested substantial resources to increase study abroad participation with the expectation that students who live and learn in the midst of another culture for an extended period of time will develop intercultural awareness, sensitivity, and language and communication skills that they could not acquire through other educational mechanisms available on campus (ACE, 2002; Green, Luu, and Burris, 2008; NAFSA, 2003).

While these efforts seem to have produced modest growth in study abroad participation rates, the beneficial effects of study abroad participation on intercultural competence and other proclaimed outcomes, while generally positive, are less clear and in some cases may be more a popular narrative than an empirically grounded claim. Some of this uncertainty about outcomes is due to methodological weaknesses in prior research (Pascarella and Terenzini, 2005), the subtle conversion of fervently advocated beliefs into presumed fact (Woolf, 2007), and policy priorities among international education administrators and study abroad programs that have emphasized boosting participation rates over ensuring educational quality (Vande Berg, 2003, 2007).

This chapter reviews the expansive body of research on the impact of study abroad on a variety of educational and developmental outcomes. It is divided into five sections:

1. Intercultural competence and the impact of study abroad on outcomes associated with intercultural competence and global perspectives.
2. The impact of study abroad on other educational and developmental outcomes.
3. The impact on general academic outcomes.
4. Effects on career.
5. Methodological issues related to determining study abroad outcomes.

As we note at the end of this chapter, studies on study abroad vary widely in scope, sample sizes, methods, and ability to control for important variables that might affect outcomes. Another complicating factor is that some authors consider intercultural competence as an integrated competence, while others study components of the broader concept. It is impossible to include every study in this monograph. We have done our best to highlight those that are illustrative of the major trends.

Intercultural Competence and Global Perspectives

Participating in study abroad has long been associated with development across a range of cognitive, psychosocial, and interpersonal domains. The educational goals of study abroad participation are often described as a combination of intercultural awareness, sensitivity, knowledge, and communication skills that, when taken together, clearly rely on an interdependence between multiple developmental domains (Deardorff, 2004). King and Baxter Magolda (1996, 2005) have also argued that these various domains of development—psychosocial, cognitive, identity, moral—are best understood as an integrated whole. The interwoven nature of these domains is poignantly exemplified by intercultural competence—a primary intended educational outcome of study abroad participation (Commission on the Abraham Lincoln Study Abroad Fellowship Program, 2005; Fulbright, 1989; Hoffa, 2007; Hoffa and DePaul,

2010; NAFSA, 2003; National Task Force on Undergraduate Education Abroad, 1990). Unfortunately, clearly defining and measuring intercultural competence has proven difficult. As the construct has been identified as an essential capacity for personal and professional success both domestically and internationally, a consensus definition has begun to emerge that provides an opportunity to assess elements of intercultural competence as an educational outcome of college (Deardorff, 2009). Because intercultural competence is such an important and frequently stated outcome of study abroad, it is important to discuss the concept before exploring intercultural competence outcomes.

Intercultural Competence[6]

Intercultural competence refers to the successful engagement or collaboration toward a single or shared set of goals between individuals or groups who do not share the same cultural origins or background. These cultural differences can arise from any combination of factors including racial, ethnic, socioeconomic, religious, and national differences. Individuals or groups demonstrating intercultural competence are able in a given situation to find "common purpose through mutually coordinated communication across cultures and languages" (Spitzberg and Changnon, 2009, p. 2). Attempts to define intercultural competence have generated increasingly divergent approaches that have made it difficult to reach a consensus among scholars.

In a recent meta-analysis that reviewed both definitions and developmental models of intercultural competence, Spitzberg and Changnon (2009) identified over 300 conceptions of the construct. After reviewing the diversity of approaches to studying intercultural competence, Spitzberg and Changnon suggest that this expanse of definitions or frameworks identify similar ingredients that can be categorized into five groups: motivation (affective, emotion), knowledge (cognitive), skills (behavior, actional), context (situation, environment, culture, relationship, function), and outcomes (perceived appropriateness or effectiveness, satisfaction, understanding, attraction, intimacy, assimilation, task achievement) (p. 7). Moreover, Spitzberg and Changnon found that in most cases these conceptualizations differed more in terminology than in substance, concluding that "many conceptual wheels are being reinvented at the expense of legitimate progress" (p. 45) toward a common definition that would better facilitate development of instruments or methodologies to measure the construct and test its validity.

In an effort to move toward a broadly accepted definition of intercultural competence and thereby allow institutions to better assess educational efforts toward intercultural competence, Deardorff (2004) conducted a two-pronged study that included a survey of international education administrators regarding institutional internationalization efforts and a Delphi approach to developing a consensus definition among an international panel of twenty-three intercultural relations experts. Deardorff found substantial overlap among scholars and international education administrators in conceptualizing intercultural competence and organized those findings into a four-part process model (2006, p. 256). These four parts are divided into two stages: individual and interaction. The individual stage encompasses two sets of attitudes or attributes. The first includes a set of attitudes including respect for or valuing other cultures, openness without judgment to intercultural learning and to people from other cultures, and a curiosity for discovery that can tolerate ambiguity during the process of exploration. The second includes an interrelated set of knowledge comprehension and interactive skills. The critical aspects of knowledge and comprehension include cultural self-awareness, a deep understanding and knowledge of culture that includes contexts, the role and impact of culture on differing worldviews, culture-specific information, and sociolinguistic awareness. The interactive skills include the ability to listen, observe, and interpret as well as analyze, evaluate, and relate knowledge gained in one setting to circumstances in a new setting.

The interaction stage is also composed of two stages: internal outcomes and external outcomes. The internal outcomes describe the development of several psychological traits including adaptability to different communication styles and behaviors or new cultural environments, both cognitive and emotional flexibility in selecting and using appropriate communication styles and behaviors, the development of an increasingly nuanced ethnorelative view, and an increased sense of empathy across cultural differences. Finally, the desired external outcome was defined as "behaving and communicating effectively and appropriately based upon one's intercultural knowledge, skills, and attitudes to achieve one's goals to some degree" (Deardorff, 2006, p. 254).

While the external outcome described in this model is undoubtedly influenced by the social context within which the interchange occurs (and therefore outside the control of the individual), each of the three prior stages taken together (as situated in Deardorff's process model) represent the attitudes, values, and attributes necessary to demonstrate intercultural competence. These capacities closely match the culminating traits of each of the three multidimensional domains proposed in King and Baxter Magolda's (2005) developmental model of intercultural maturity. For a more extended discussion of the relationship between Deardorff's model and that of King and Baxter Magolda, see Salisbury (2011).

In summary, intercultural competence and the developmental process toward intercultural competence can be understood along three vectors:

1. Cognitive development, which allows for a relativistic appreciation of similarities and differences among diverse individuals.
2. Psychosocial (or intrapersonal) development, which facilitates increasing comfort when engaged in interactions with diverse others.
3. Interpersonal development, which empowers one to seek out diverse interactions through experiences that highlight, celebrate, or examine differences among diverse individuals or groups.

Study Abroad and Intercultural Competence

The assertion that studying abroad improves intercultural competence is grounded in the contact hypothesis. Allport (1954) proposed that prejudice held by one group toward another group could be reduced if individuals from both groups participated in sustained interpersonal contact. Subsequent research testing this hypothesis under a variety of conditions identified several caveats under which intergroup relations were most likely to reduce prejudice (Hewstone and Brown, 1986). These conditions include equality of status during contact, a social context that supports equality between groups, collaborative engagement toward a shared goal, opportunity to develop the level of intimacy necessary to contradict previously held stereotypes, and the support of applicable authority figures. In a meta-analysis of 713 independent samples from 515 studies distributed across almost fifty years of research, Pettigrew and Tropp (2006) found strong support for the contact hypothesis.

While the contact hypothesis originated within the context of improving relations between domestic racial groups, Amir (1969) reviewed and synthesized efforts to apply the contact hypothesis to improve inter-ethnic and international relations. Amir found that, although the majority of findings support the assertion that contact between groups of differing ethnic origins or nationalities was likely to produce change in the attitudes of both groups toward the other, the conditions under which this contact occurs are significantly influential in determining the direction, or intensity, of the attitudinal change. In addition to the conditions outlined by Allport (1954) that might encourage positive attitudinal change, Amir noted several conditions specific to interethnic or international interactions that might inhibit positive change or even increase prejudice. These unfavorable conditions include when the contact is "unpleasant, involuntary or tension laden," when one group is "in a state of frustration (i.e., inadequate personality structure, recent defeat or failure, economic depression, etc.)" potentially leading to ethnic "scapegoating," [blaming local difficulties or inequality on another specific racial or ethnic group] and when the two groups find each other's moral or ethical values objectionable (p. 339). In the presence of one or more unfavorable conditions, sustained contact could increase or intensify prejudice rather than reduce it.

Intercultural Competence Outcomes of Study Abroad

Clearly, the cognitive, intrapersonal, and interpersonal capacities necessary to exhibit intercultural competence—sensitivity to cultural differences, awareness of sociohistorical cultural contexts, adaptability and flexibility to view cultural differences and contextual circumstances through an informed ethnorelative lens, and the empathy to seek deeper understanding while withholding judgment—are all attributes that could mitigate the presence of the unfavorable conditions listed above and thereby increase the likelihood of a positive cross-cultural outcome. Not surprisingly, study abroad advocates and international education scholars have repeatedly sought to demonstrate the positive effect of studying abroad on intercultural competence (and various components of it) under the presumption that the conditions for intergroup contact during a study abroad experience are ideal for reducing prejudice, developing intercultural competency skills, and improving relations across cultural, ethnic, and/or national differences (Sell, 1983; Pascarella and Terenzini, 2005).

A few exceptions notwithstanding (Kalunian, 1997, as cited in Pascarella and Terenzini, 2005; Patterson, 2006; Wilkinson, 1998a, 2000), researchers have repeatedly found that students who study abroad demonstrate positive change on several aspects of intercultural competence upon return to their home campuses. Although the language describing the outcome of interest varies across this body of work, numerous single-institution, small-sample studies have investigated the effect of studying abroad on three broad aspects of intercultural competence: (1) the respondent's view of the host culture or country, (2) the respondent's global perspective or world-mindedness, and (3) the respondent's intercultural awareness or sensitivity. Findings from these studies seem to suggest that students who study abroad develop a more positive view of the host culture (Bicknese, 1974; Carlson and Widaman, 1988; Cushner and Karim, 2004; Nash, 1976), expand their global perspective or world-mindedness (Chieffo and Griffiths, 2004; Cushner and Mahon, 2002; Douglas and Jones-Rikkers, 2001; Golay, 2006), and increase their intercultural awareness and sensitivity (Anderson, Lawton, Rexeisen, and Hubbard, 2006; Black and Duhon, 2006; Pedersen, 2009; Shaheen, 2004; Williams, 2005).

For example, a key outcome expected from study abroad is an increased sense of open-mindedness and/or global mindedness. Defining open-mindedness as "the ability to effectively embrace diverse cultures and function across key skill areas" (p. 175), Clarke, Flaherty, Wright, and McMillen (2009) found that study abroad students demonstrated higher levels of open-mindedness than students who had not studied abroad. Hadis (2005), Kitsantas and Meyers (2001), and Kitsantas (2004) also found that the majority of students who studied abroad came away with a greater openness to new ideas. Students who were more open-minded had fewer adaptation problems and were more resilient to feelings of depression, and reported being more independent (Hadis, 2005; Kitsantas and Meyers, 2001). No mention in these studies was given to the fact that these finding might be due to selection bias. Instead it was assumed that studying abroad led to the gains.

Study abroad participants also demonstrate increases in global-mindedness, an overall awareness of world issues, and a sense of how local issues relate to world issues (Hadis, 2005). Hadis (2005) found that over 90 percent of students studied had a "deepened interest in world affairs" (p. 61) compared to pre-sojourn levels. This connection to the global environment was observed to be significantly different than the experience of the typical college student (Hadis, 2005). Kitsantas (2004) noted changes in student attitudes similar to those found by Hadis. Students, as well as developing a new and improved approach toward global affairs, showed a heightened sense of empathy and respect for the country where they sojourned, and a heightened sense of global understanding (Kitsantas, 2004; Kitsantas and Meyers, 2001) and global engagement (Clarke, Flaherty, Wright, and McMillen, 2009). Study abroad students were further found to have a greater appreciation for multiple cultures, not just the study abroad host culture, as well as how their home culture impacts the global environment (Clarke, Flaherty, Wright, and McMillen, 2009).

Global-mindedness is often considered in conjunction with indicators of sensitivity (Kitsantas, 2004; Kitsantas and Meyers, 2001). As previously noted, students with a study abroad experience were able to effectively empathize with other cultures (Kitsantas, 2004; Kitsantas and Meyers, 2001). Clarke, Flaherty, Wright, and McMillen (2009) defined sensitivity toward other cultures in terms of ethnocentrism (insensitivity) and ethnorelativism (sensitivity). Students who had participated in a study abroad program showed significantly higher levels of ethnorelativisim, and were therefore "better prepared to understand life choices and behaviors within another cultural context" (p. 177) than student with no experience abroad. Students with study abroad experience were able to reflect on sensitivity to cultures that they had little to no interaction with (Clarke, Flaherty, Wright, and McMillen, 2009). Furthermore, because of an experience abroad, students were able to shift between cultures by selecting the "aspects of a culture befitting a particular situation" (p. 178) in order to function multiculturally (Clarke, Flaherty, Wright, and McMillen, 2009).

In addition, students may be more willing to critically examine foreign policy and other national and international issues after a study abroad experience (Dolby, 2007) and are also more interested in international affairs after studying abroad than before (Carlson, Burn, Useem, and Yachimovicz, 1990). Even though students may gain a heightened sense of global awareness as well as ability to critique the positive and negative of the United States,

Clarke, Flaherty, Wright, and McMillen (2009) concluded that students may not equate that awareness with an increased sense "of responsibility to the global community, nor a greater interest in the 'good of the world'" (p. 176). The authors concluded that students will need further and more direct ethics guidance if global responsibility, not just global awareness, is a desirable outcome.

Even short-term programs seem to have positive effects on these components of intercultural competence (Chieffo and Griffiths, 2009). Compared with students who took a comparable course on the home campus, students who studied abroad for a month were more cognizant of cultural differences, reported much broader learning gains on a wide range of topics such as tolerance, appreciation of another culture, and language issues, than were the students who remained on campus. The stay-at-home students were far more focused on academic gains (Chieffo and Griffiths, 2004). Nearly one-third returned from study abroad with a new sense of their own culture and the role of the United States in global affairs. This is an important finding, as short-term programs have become the dominant form of study abroad.

A possible side effect of increased open-mindedness and global-mindedness may be oversensitivity about one's own culture. Research suggests that students gain a heightened, more finely tuned (critical) sensitivity to characteristics and platitudes of the American culture, particularly evident upon return. Hadis (2005) broadly described this sensitivity as "reverse culture shock" (p. 62) as a process of questioning and discarding the preconceptions and learned traits of one's home society based on the experience gained from a trip abroad. A majority of students felt that they experience reverse cultural shock at some point after returning to the United States—that is, returning students started thinking critically about things they had taken for granted.

Three large-scale studies have examined the effect of study abroad on aspects of intercultural competence in the last several decades. The Study Abroad Evaluation Project (SAEP) sought to identify differences between study abroad participants and non-participants as well as whether or not the experience significantly influenced change on several aspects of an international perspective (Carlson, Burn, Useem, and Yachimowicz, 1990). Examining data from 358 students across four institutions (251 studied abroad, 157 remained on campus), this study found that the study abroad students scored higher on both pre- and posttest measures of international perspective than a control group of students who remained on campus during the junior year. However, the gap between the experimental and control groups' scores did not change significantly, suggesting that the study abroad students' relative advantage in international perspective scores was not a function of study abroad participation.

More recently, the Georgetown Consortium Project examined data from 1,297 students (1163 studied abroad, 134 remained on campus) to ascertain differences in gains on intercultural sensitivity (Vande Berg, Connor-Linton, and Paige, 2009). Chi-square tests of pre- and posttest scores indicated that the study abroad participants made significant gains on a measure of intercultural sensitivity while the control students' score did not change. Although this study also found that gains differed across a variety of demographic and program design variations, the analysis did not include whether the statistically significant gains made by the study abroad students held in the presence of controls for other pre-experience differences.

A more rigorous examination of study abroad participation's impact on intercultural competence involved an analysis of data from the 2006 cohort of the Wabash National Study of Liberal Arts Education (Salisbury, 2011). Findings from 1,593 students across 17 institutions revealed that, even in the presence of a battery of controls assessing demographic characteristics, precollege attitudes, institutional context, academic pursuits, college experiences, and a propensity score to account for potential selection bias, study abroad participation generated a statistically significant positive effect on intercultural competence gains. However, further analysis indicated that this effect was restricted to one subscale of the overall dependent measure—an inclination toward diverse contact, and did not appear across the two other subscales—comfort with diversity and relativistic appreciation. Salisbury (2011) interpreted these findings to suggest that, while study abroad might potentially play a role in intercultural competence development, it might not be the transformational educational experience that many claimed study abroad to be. Furthermore, since his study found that other campus-based diversity experiences generated comparatively larger effect sizes across more of the constituent subscale measures of intercultural competence than study abroad participation,

Salisbury suggested that perhaps institutions might invest resources in other, less expensive diversity experiences as a more efficient means of developing intercultural competence in students.

Other Educational and Developmental Outcomes

Study abroad advocates have long argued that the experience of living and learning abroad has a unique effect on many of the broad educational outcomes historically associated with a liberal arts education. Study abroad participation has been linked with aspects of psychosocial—often called personal—development (Gmelch, 1997; Gullahorn and Gullahorn, 1966; Kauffmann, 1983; Milstein, 2005), identity development (Dolby, 2004; Talburt and Stewart, 1999), moral or values development (Jurgens and McAuliffe, 2004; Lindsey, 2005; Ryan and Twibell, 2000), intellectual development (Barrutia, 1971; McKeown, 2009; Zhai and Scheer, 2002), and holistic development conceptualized as self-authorship (Braskamp, Braskamp, and Merrill, 2009; Du, 2007).

For example, using a pretest-posttest design, Braskamp, Braskamp, and Merrill (2009) sought to identify changes in global perspectives among students from five institutions enrolled in ten different one-semester study abroad programs. The authors conclude that study abroad participants had higher posttest scores on knowledge (of other cultures), intrapersonal (awareness of one's own identity and respect for others), and interpersonal (interactions with others who are different and social concern for others). The only dimension on which posttest scores were not higher was that of knowing (understanding role of cultural context).

These findings led them to conclude that "education abroad is an effective educational experience for students, if the desired goal of an education abroad experience is to help students to develop holistically and globally. Students progressed in all three domains of global learning and development from the beginning to the end of the education abroad experience" (p. 110).

Identity

Several authors have investigated the effects of study abroad on identity development, specifically on what it means to be American. Dolby (2007) and

Hadis (2005) found that students, upon returning from an overseas journey, have learned a great deal about themselves as students, as individuals, as American citizens and as global citizens.

The question of how study abroad affects one's own identity as American is a somewhat understudied as we usually think about the goals of study abroad to be learning about the "other." Interviewing twelve students who studied abroad in a wide range of destinations, Souders (2006) explored identity negotiation of these students during the sojourn and upon return. These students engaged in what Souders called "othering," both internal and external. Upon return from their semester or yearlong sojourn, students saw themselves as clearly more international than their classmates who had not studied abroad. For some students, part of the external "othering" involved seeing themselves in comparison to less desirable Americans, identifying both positive and negative stereotypes of Americanness, as well as seeing themselves, post sojourn, as atypical Americans.

Dolby (2007) and Clarke, Flaherty, Wright, and McMillen (2009) found similar results when examining how students viewed themselves as Americans in the post-9/11 world. Students were more critical of their American culture during their sojourn and upon their return. Because of public opinion toward the Afghanistan and Iraq wars, some students were also hypersensitive to being viewed as "American" while abroad and therefore went out of their way to "fit in" with the local culture (Dolby, 2007; Clarke, Flaherty, Wright, and McMillen, 2009). This hypersensitivity to being American was realized by students just prior to and during the first few weeks of their sojourn. Souders (2006) even found students adopting what he calls the "Canadian of Convenience" (pp. 31–32) identity to avoid negative attention due to being American. These reflections, even negative ones, suggest that studying abroad helps students to define themselves and their culture in relation to the culture that they are experiencing. These reflections seem to indicate that studying abroad is, at least to some extent, meeting the goal of making American students more culturally aware.

These "identity" outcomes of studying abroad help students communicate interpersonally, define their beliefs and realize that they were more competent than previously thought (Younes and Asay, 2003). The majority of students in Hadis's (2005) study indicated that they were no longer reliant on adults to make decisions for them after sojourning. According to Jessup-Anger (2008), sojourning helped male and female students identify, in both positive and negative ways, with their respective genders by observing how other cultures viewed and treated females and males. Studying abroad forced students to reexamine how they reviewed their personal strengths and weaknesses (Younes and Asay, 2003).

Intellectual/Cognitive Development

Despite difficulties linking study abroad to grades and disciplinary outcomes, attention has been directed to intellectual or cognitive development as an outcome of study abroad. Such development is widely accepted as occurring during the college years so the question is whether students who study abroad achieve greater growth in intellectual development than those who do not. The aspects of intellectual/cognitive development measured in relation to study abroad are varied, and consequently this section reflects a sort of potpourri of outcomes.

Intellectual Development. In an attempt to assess the effect of study abroad on intellectual development, McKeown (2009) studied 226 participants in semester-long study abroad programs from eight colleges. He administered the Measure of Intellectual Development (MID) predeparture and postsojourn. McKeown was able to control for a variety of experiential variables likely to affect study abroad outcomes such as gender, language of host country, degree of cultural immersion measured by where and with whom students studied while abroad and where and with whom they lived, student activities while abroad, and finally whether they had traveled abroad before. He concludes that "on most variables important to the study abroad profession, namely, program structure, language, and degree of cultural immersion, there were no statistically significant differences in intellectual development from pre- to post-program" (p. 98). Rather, the only variable he found to be important was what he calls the "first-time effect." Students for whom the study abroad experience he studied was the first such experience began with lower levels of intellectual development than their peers who had traveled and studied abroad but by the end had achieved equivalent levels of intellectual development (p. 98). This led him to conclude that the first study abroad experience is the most beneficial. Since all of the participants in McKeown's study were on semester-long programs, these gains should not be generalized to short-term programs or to yearlong programs. In fact, he argues that even one semester may be too short a period for students to show much growth in a complex phenomenon such as intellectual development.

Our review suggests that study abroad students do seem to advance on various measures associated with intellectual development such as open-mindedness and ethnorelativism even if they did not in McKeown's study.

Academic Interest. Studies by Dolby (2004, 2007), Hadis (2005), and Vande Berg (2007) found that students were more engaged academically upon their return from a trip overseas. According to Hadis, students generally return from an experience abroad with a "higher than average curiosity and interest in academic matters"(p. 57). Study abroad students may also have new academic interests upon their return (Carlson, Burn, Useem, and Yachimovicz, 1990). Furthermore, students emerge from a study abroad experience placing a higher value on their overall educational experience—including K–12 and higher education (Dolby, 2005). Hadis also noted that the majority of students returning from a study abroad experience are more interested "in studying for the 'pleasure of knowledge,' than to get a good grade" (p. 63). Laubscher (1994) notes that students perceived that they had made significant gains in a number of areas as a result of study abroad and some of the nonacademic activities associated with study abroad: "maturity, independence, self-reliance, and tolerance of ambiguity" (p. 105) as well as cultural sensitivity.

General Academic Outcomes

As study abroad participation rates have increased and diversified across academic disciplines, researchers from a wide range of academic fields have increasingly endeavored to demonstrate the educational benefits of studying abroad and to dispel claims that study abroad will have adverse effects (Hamir, 2011; Lewin, 2009; McKeown, 2009; Savicki, 2008). International education scholars have linked study abroad participation with several indicators of general academic success including graduation rates (Hamir, 2011; Posey, 2003; Sutton and Rubin, 2010), time to degree (Flash, 1999; Hamir, 2011; Ingraham and Peterson, 2004), retention (Kasravi, 2009; Metzger, 2006; Young, 2003), and grade point average (Posey, 2003; Sutton and Rubin, 2010; Thomas and McMahon, 1998). Not surprisingly, foreign language scholars have repeatedly found study abroad to positively affect second language acquisition (Brecht, Davidson, and Ginsberg, 1995; Churchill and DuFon, 2006; Freed, 1995; Magnan and Back, 2007). Moreover, researchers have also found study abroad to be correlated with increased engagement in other educationally beneficial activities during college (Gonyea, 2008) as well as specific career choices after college (Armstrong, 1984; Mistretta, 2008; Norris and Gillespie, 2009; Wallace, 1999). In the section that follows, we expand on some of these findings.

We should note that much of the recent research on this group of outcomes has come from recently completed dissertations and thus the following section is heavily based on research that has not as yet been published in refereed journals.

Grades

In one of the few studies attempting to understand the relationship between grades and study abroad, Thomas and McMahon (1998) examined the records of 1,600 University of California study abroad students on yearlong programs in Israel and Western Europe. They found that predeparture grade point averages were strongly correlated with grade point averages attained during the study abroad year, supporting the use of predeparture grade point average as a selection criterion. Interestingly, they also found that students' grades improved between the time of application for study abroad and the actual departure. Not surprisingly predeparture language ability was strongly correlated with academic outcomes in non-English-speaking countries. White females (the majority of study abroad participants) had higher predeparture grade point averages than white males, but white males performed better academically while abroad. Moreover, students admitted exceptionally (that is, with lower than the required predeparture academic scores) performed acceptably in study abroad.

Assessing the impact of study abroad on college grade point average poses particular challenges, which is likely why it is seldom used as an outcome measure (Merva, 2003). For example, translating a host institution's grading scheme to performance on the home institution's scale can be difficult. In other cases, students choose not to transfer courses if grades are lower than they would like (Merva, 2003). Moreover, a focus on grades may discourage students from choosing to study abroad (Hadis, 2005).

Graduation Rates

To counteract the criticism that study abroad delays graduation, studies about the relationship of study abroad to graduation rates and time to degree are emerging, mostly in yet unpublished dissertations based on single-institution studies at large, public research universities. The emerging consensus is pretty clear: study abroad does not negatively impact time to degree or graduation rates, and it may actually positively affect both. In her dissertation, Flash (1999) investigated the question of participation in study abroad and its effect on time to degree and found that overall participation in an overseas educational experience did not result in a later graduation date regardless of gender, destination, program length, or major. Of those research participants who did report a delay in their graduation, most admitted to being aware that going abroad would extend their time to degree, and the delay was considered to be minor and not a deterrent to participation. Similarly, Hamir (2011) in a study of graduation rates of first time freshmen at the University of Texas found that students who studied abroad were more likely to have graduated at five-, six-, and eight-year postenrollment markers than students who did not study abroad. These findings were independent of other variables that affect graduation rates, such as grade point average, gender, race/ethnicity, and so on. That is, it was not because of higher predeparture grade point averages that study abroad participants graduated at higher rates. Hamir concludes that participation in study abroad increased a participant's likelihood of graduating in four years by 14.3 percent, even though study abroad was not a significant predictor of graduating in four years when controlling for demographic characteristics compared to nonparticipants. The effect of study abroad seemed to increase at the five- and six-year markers. Additionally, study abroad did not delay time to graduation. Like Hamir (2011), Sutton and Rubin (2010) found that four-, five-, and six-year graduation rates for study abroad participants in the Georgia Learning Outcomes of Students Studying Abroad Research Initiative (GLOSSARI) project were higher than for those who remained stateside, and this held true across gender, race, and SAT score. They calculated that study abroad participants were 16 percent more likely to graduate in four years than those who did not participate.

Hamir's study is one of the few to examine the effects of study abroad program type on time to degree. Surprisingly she found that participants in faculty-led study abroad programs took longer to graduate than those who participated in affiliated or exchange programs. This finding seemed somewhat contradictory to another of her findings: that long-term program participants had lower graduation rates at all post-enrollment markers and took longer to graduate than mid-length or short-term participants. Finally, Hamir also found that UT-Austin study abroad participants who went abroad as underclassmen had lower degree completion rates at all postenrollment markers compared to study abroad participants who were juniors or seniors when they studied abroad. This suggests that pushing students to study abroad early in their academic careers may be counterproductive. However, she does provide some evidence that study abroad helped UT-Austin students with lower grade point averages graduate in a timely manner, lending support to Thomas and McMahon's (1998) finding that some students with low grade point averages can succeed in study abroad.

Posey (2003) adds to our understanding by examining the relationship of study abroad to degree completion at a variety of postsecondary degree classifications including associate, bachelor, master, law, and specialist. He discovered that study abroad participants generally graduated at a higher rate than nonparticipants for all but the associate's degree. In terms of time to degree, a slight difference was found in favor of study abroad participants. That is, students who participated in study abroad on average graduated in less time than their nonparticipant counterparts, although this finding was not significant. Globally speaking, Posey (2003) asserts that participation in study abroad appears to have minimal effect on time to degree.

Several studies are more equivocal about the relationship of study abroad and graduation measures. Although study abroad seemed to neither delay graduation nor negatively affect graduation rates for students at the University of Minnesota Twin Cities, Malmgren and Galvin (2008) were unwilling to attribute this to study abroad. They argue that a host of other factors, in addition to study abroad, could potentially affect rates of graduation. Interestingly, Malmgren and Galvin also found that study abroad participation positively affected graduation rates of minority and at-risk students, a finding consistent with Hamir's (2011) findings. Ingraham and Peterson's (2004) findings from an evaluation of study abroad at Michigan State University also suggest that the relationship between study abroad and graduation is somewhat less clear. Their data showed that "on average, study abroad participants enroll for more terms before graduating than do non-participants *but* that they take less time to graduate" (p. 98). That is, study abroad participants graduate in less time than nonparticipants perhaps because of the various designs of study abroad programs that can be completed over the summer.

Although the research shows no clear negative effect of study abroad on various graduation measures, there is some evidence that students believe it will and thus decide not to participate for this reason (Hamir, 2011; Malmgren and Galvin, 2008). Malmgren and Galvin (2008) asked students, faculty members, and advisors the question: "How important is delay in graduation in considering study abroad?" The respondents, student and administration alike, agreed that it was either somewhat, very, or the most important factor in deciding whether to study internationally. This suggests that it is very important to provide students with the data showing that study abroad does not delay or negatively affect graduation but that some careful planning may be necessary to ensure that this does not happen. It is also the case that most studies examining the relationship between study abroad and time to degree or graduation rates are not able to control for variables such as motivation or other characteristics that might be differentiate those who do study abroad from those who do not on factors related to graduating in a timely manner.

Language Proficiency
Improving foreign language proficiency has long been a major goal of study abroad. As Freed (1998) notes, this is based on the assumption that the optimal environment for learning a language involves some combination of formal

classroom study and immersion in the target language. This assumption has led to the popular myth among students, faculty, and parents that by merely studying abroad, one will become fluent in the target language (Freed, 1998). The results of dozens of studies have shown that the effects of study abroad on language acquisition are more nuanced, although generally positive. Readers particularly interested in the effects of study abroad on language acquisition are directed to two thorough literature reviews on the topic: "An Overview of Issues and Research in Language Learning in a Study Abroad Setting" by Barbara F. Freed (1998) and "Evolving Threads in Study Abroad Research" by Eton Churchill and Margaret A. Dufon (2006).

Freed (1998) summarized her extensive review with the following sketch:

> *Those who have been abroad appear to speak with greater ease and confidence, expressed in part by a greater abundance of speech, spoken at a faster rate and characterized by fewer dysfluent-sounding pauses. As a group, they tend to reformulate their speech to express more complicated and abstract thoughts, display a wider range of communicative strategies and a broader repertoire of styles. It is equally clear that their linguistic identities extend beyond the expected acquisition of oral skills to new self-realization in the social world of literacy [p. 50].*

She goes on to note that research is far less abundant about accuracy of language used but that early results suggest there may be a plateau—advanced learners do not make significant gains abroad.

The literature suggests that the study abroad context has a significant effect on language skill development and interacts with individual differences and experiences to affect language proficiency gains. Through qualitative investigations of the study abroad experience, researchers have learned, for example, that the amount and nature of immersion may vary and be less than imagined, or that harassment and fear for safety may constrict interaction of female students with the host culture (Brecht, Davidson and Ginsberg, 1995; Polanyi, 1995).

Reviewing research that appeared subsequent to the Freed review, Churchill and Dufon (2006) draw some methodological and substantive conclusions about the relationship of study abroad to language learning. With respect to substantive gains, they note that even short programs can lead to some gains; however, longer programs have greater benefits in pragmatics, the increased ability to use language in functionally appropriate ways. That said, Churchill and Dufon conclude from their review that at best, even the more advanced students can only approach native fluency. While by definition one would expect that those with lower predeparture levels would stand to gain the most, it is clear from the research that language development is mediated by complex interactions between the individual learner and the particular host country environment they find themselves in. Freed argues that one of the important implications of research on the relation of study abroad to foreign language proficiency is that U.S. colleges and universities must address the need to help study abroad students maintain their hard-won language skills when they return from study abroad.

Disciplinary Knowledge

A wide variety of researchers suggest that understanding the relationship between academic achievement and study abroad is essential for selecting students who can best benefit from study abroad, for preparing students for studying overseas (Hadis, 2005; Merva, 2003; Thomas and McMahon, 1998; Vande Berg, 2007), and for assessing their sojourn (Vande Berg, 2007). Despite the fact that study abroad has been linked with credits toward a U.S. college degree, very little interest has been devoted to studying academic disciplinary gains from study abroad beyond language acquisition. This is due in part to the fact that acquiring disciplinary knowledge has been at best a secondary goal to achieving language, cultural knowledge, intercultural, and personal development goals. As McKeown (2009) notes, assessing academic impact of study abroad becomes even more complicated with the rise of wildly diverse study abroad options and outcomes.

General Learning Outcomes

Results from the initial phase of the GLOSSARI project (Sutton and Rubin, 2004) indicated that a sample of students who studied abroad demonstrated greater outcomes on a variety of what they label as general academic outcomes than a sample of students who did not (Sutton and Rubin, 2004). They conclude that students who study abroad reported higher levels of functional knowledge of how to live and interact in other countries, knowledge of global interdependence, knowledge of cultural relativism, and knowledge of world geography. These findings held even when controlling for self-reported grade point average; however, there were some differences by major. For example, education majors who studied abroad scored lower on knowledge of global interdependence than other majors, while business majors scored lower on measures of cultural relativism. They conclude that study abroad did not affect several important outcomes, namely, communication skills.

Sutton and Rubin's recent findings reinforce those of Carlson, Burn, Useem, and Yachimovicz's classic 1990 study. Carlson and colleagues examined changes in yearlong study abroad students on a number of general academic outcomes and also compared study abroad students with a group of comparable students who did not study abroad. The groups of outcomes examined include international understanding, which had both cognitive and affective dimensions, academic issues (problems abroad, learning styles, and ways of thinking and learning), self-efficacy, professional goals, and satisfaction. (They also included foreign language gains but we will not include those here.) Perhaps surprisingly, Carlson and colleagues found differences between the study abroad group and the comparison group on only two outcomes: cultural interest and "peace and cooperation." Neither group changed significantly between test administrations. Study abroad students became less domestically oriented, while domestic students did not change. The authors found few other academic differences other than the study abroad participants perceived themselves to be higher on abstract thinking than the comparison group, but both increased over the time span of the study. Study abroad did not seem to positively affect self-efficacy although Milstein (2005) found that study abroad for individuals in a Japanese exchange and teaching program did grow in self-efficacy.

Effects of Program Duration

As Dwyer (2004) notes, "conventional wisdom in the study abroad field has held that more is better" (p. 151), that longer study abroad will result in greater benefits than short-term programs. Given the growth of short-term programs, understanding effects of program duration becomes an important question. We found few studies that intentionally included program duration as a variable. Dwyer used data from an IES study of its alumni designed to determine relationships between program features and outcomes. In this particular study, program length options included full-year, fall semester, spring semester, and summer term. Shorter program effects were not assessed. In short, in all outcome areas—general, academic, intercultural, career, and personal—studying abroad for a full year resulted in greater perceived effects than did participation for shorter periods of time.

Career and Other Long-Term Effects

Assessing the effect of study abroad on a host of longer-term outcomes, including career, is challenging. Studies that have taken on these questions largely rely on retrospective assessments of the impact study abroad has had on participants. Building on Carlson, Burn, Useem, and Yachimovicz's (1990) SAEP study, two recent large-scale studies have examined the effect of study abroad on longer-term outcomes: the IES Abroad Fifty-Year Alumni Survey (Norris and Gillespie, 2009) and the Study Abroad for Global Engagement project (SAGE) at the University of Minnesota (University of Minnesota, n.d.).

Carlson, Burn, Useem, and Yachimovicz (1990) found that a sample of study abroad alumni/ae had earned bachelor's degrees and a sizeable percentage of both men and women had advanced degrees or further education. They categorized their respondents into maximizers (forty-five of seventy-six), who somehow integrated European study abroad into career values and employment practices, and minimizers (thirty-one of seventy-six). For this group, study abroad was valued but not directly relevant to work life. Carlson, Burn, Useem, and Yachimovicz's findings received more recent support from Paige and others (2009). In their retrospective study of 6,391 alumni of study abroad programs at twenty-two colleges and universities, Paige and others found that 60 percent of the sample had advanced degrees and nearly 38 percent reported working in an internationally oriented career.

Conducted in 2002, the IES fifty-year alumni/ae survey was sent to 17,000 alumni of IES study abroad programs. As in other studies of long-term effects (Carlson, Burn, Useem, and Yachimovicz, 1990; Wallace, 1999), Norris and Gillespie (2008) found that a majority of respondents agreed that study abroad had influenced their career by enhancing interest, increasing foreign language skills, and giving them important job-related skills. However, a much smaller percentage of alumni (17 percent) said that study abroad influenced whether or not they worked abroad, worked for a multinational corporation, or changed career plans. When Norris and Gillespie analyzed the data by decade, they concluded that more recent study abroad graduates were more likely than earlier generations to relate working abroad or for a multinational organization to their study abroad experience. Taking another approach to the question of career impact, Norris and Gillespie conclude that 48 percent of their respondents actually had some global dimension to their career (either volunteering or job). They then compare this global group with those alumni whose careers had not had a global dimension with respect to the impact of the study abroad experience. They conclude that those working globally had additional study abroad experiences and use foreign language more as compared to the domestic group. The global group was more likely to change career plans following study abroad. Various program aspects were related to having global careers: studying in a foreign language, participating in longer programs, taking courses from the host university, having an internship while abroad, having lived with a host family, and maintaining contacts in the host culture.

Norris and Gillespie (2008) conclude that:

> *All of these programming data illustrated that students who study abroad longer select programs taught exclusively in a foreign language, enroll in host university courses, participate in internships, and live with host families are more likely to develop international aspects to their careers. This suggests a continuum of decision making that leads many education abroad students to integrate their cross-cultural knowledge, skills, and interests into their professional lives [p. 393].*

The SAGE project, a multiyear study funded by the U.S. Department of Education, explores the reported long-term impact of study abroad on global engagement on 6,000 alumni/ae from twenty-two colleges and universities, defined as including attributes such as civic engagement, knowledge production, philanthropy, social entrepreneurship, and something that they label voluntary simplicity (Jon and Fry, 2009). The value-laden nature of their outcome measures notwithstanding, the authors conclude that alumni who had studied abroad reported that study abroad influenced their behavior on most of the behaviors except (and perhaps surprisingly) philanthropy. Over half of the respondents indicated that study abroad had little influence on their volunteer work or their monetary donations.

In summary, the effects of study abroad on a wide range of variables has been studied, and while the results are generally positive, the findings are also far more nuanced and less overwhelmingly positive than the rhetoric surrounding study abroad would have us believe. Moreover, one must read the literature with a careful eye due to the methodological weaknesses of much of the literature. We now turn to a discussion of some of those weaknesses.

Methodological Weaknesses of Study Abroad Outcomes Literature

Although all of these studies assert evidence to support the claim that studying abroad uniquely influences the development of intercultural competence and other outcomes, several methodological weaknesses must be considered that may limit the validity and generalizability of any individual study. First, many studies examine a small group of students at a particular institution, comparing them to an equally small and homogeneous non-randomly assigned control group (if there is a control group at all). In most cases, these studies are also limited to students who participated in a particular study abroad program. Furthermore, some of these studies are even restricted to students in a specific major. Since each of the samples in these studies is far from nationally representative of all undergraduates, it is exceedingly difficult to generalize any of these findings to all college students who study abroad. Second, as Pascarella and Terenzini (2005) noted in their review of college impact research, none of these studies adequately accounts for the potentially confounding demographic, attitudinal, or aspirational characteristics that might systematically differentiate between students who do and do not study abroad.

Even the most extensive efforts to demonstrate the effect of study abroad on its participants' intercultural attitudes and skills suffer from notable weaknesses in design or analysis. Although the 1984–1985 Study Abroad Evaluation Project (SAEP) (Carlson, Burn, Useem, and Yachimovicz, 1990) collected data from students at multiple American institutions ($N = 4$), applied a longitudinal design, and controlled for a host of potentially confounding variables, the analysis did not account for the possibility that effects observed may have resulted from differences between the students who selected to participate in study abroad and the students who did not. In addition, the sample of student respondents came primarily from large research institutions (the control group coming almost entirely from a single large public university), thus making it difficult to generalize the findings to students at other types of institutions, especially small, private liberal arts colleges where study abroad originated and remains more deeply institutionalized. Although the study found that students who studied abroad grew in ways that the students who stayed home did not, it was impossible to know whether that growth was uniquely a function of studying abroad or rather a by-product of other observed or unobserved characteristics.

The Georgetown Consortium Project (Vande Berg, Connor-Linton, and Paige, 2009) examined gains on several outcomes regarding second language acquisition and intercultural awareness and competency development across a range of study abroad program differences using a pretest/posttest design. However, this study only analyzed mean differences between the pre- and posttest scores for the treatment and control groups without controlling for any other potentially confounding characteristics. Furthermore, the control group differed substantially from the treatment group in size and distribution across institutions, making it difficult to make confident assertions about the validity of the findings.

Finally, the GLOSSARI Project (Sutton and Rubin, 2004) endeavored to assess the effects of study abroad participation across a variety of intercultural and academic progress measures using data gathered from students at institutions throughout the University System of Georgia. However, this study failed to employ a pretest/posttest design and only controlled for GPA and academic major in its analysis, omitting any other precollege characteristics or attitudinal differences between student groups. Furthermore, the study's means of convenience sampling left open the significant possibility of sample selection bias. Although this study is currently implementing a second phase that attempts to correct for previous methodological and design weaknesses, the sampling frame continues to be students within the University System of Georgia, again making it difficult to generalize the findings to students at private institutions.

Two additional and potentially more fundamental problems undermine the validity of the existing body of research on study abroad. After reviewing the state of study abroad research almost twenty-five years ago, Church (1982) and Sell (1983) noted that the vast majority of the study abroad research to date had been constructed absent grounding in a plausible theoretical framework. Black and Mendenhall (1991) found the same to be true of the research on cross-cultural adjustment among study abroad participants. Although Pascarella and Terenzini (2005) did not assert such a stark assessment of the study abroad research involving college students, they clearly noted that the existing body of findings had failed to account for differences between students who choose to study abroad and students who choose not to study abroad. In the context of Pascarella's (1985) model for examining the impact of specific college experiences on college student educational outcomes, Pascarella and Terenzini's critique of research on undergraduate study abroad seems to mirror the conclusions of these earlier reviews. Undergraduate study abroad does not occur, nor does it function, in isolation from the larger postsecondary educational enterprise. As such, any effort to examine its impact without accounting for the potential confounding effects of this context would seem incomplete. Moreover, despite an extensive body of research demonstrating that college student development across a range of cognitive, affective, or holistic domains cannot be expected to occur at a uniform pace, in a linear fashion, or within a quantifiable time frame (Baxter Magolda, 2001; Kegan, 1982, 1994; King and Kitchener, 1994; Pascarella and Terenzini, 1991, 2005; Perry, 1970), research on the effects of study abroad has consistently operated under the assumption that any change resulting from the study abroad experience should be evident immediately upon its conclusion.

The second methodological weakness found both in the single institution studies as well as the larger scale studies is the lack of adequate accounting for factors that might systematically differentiate students who choose to study abroad from students who choose not to study abroad. Yet both descriptive data on study abroad participants as well as the few studies examining the factors that predict study abroad intent or participation have demonstrated the degree to which students who study abroad differ from those who remain on campus (Booker, 2001; Carlson, Burn, Useem, and Yachimovicz, 1990; Commission on the Abraham Lincoln Study Abroad Fellowship Program, 2005; Goldstein and Kim, 2006; IIE, 2009; Koester, 1985; NAFSA, 2003; Salisbury, Paulsen, and Pascarella, 2011; Salisbury, Umbach, Paulsen, and Pascarella, 2009; Spiering and Erickson, 2006).

Yet another weakness in study abroad outcomes research is failure to account for program characteristics (for example, Engle and Engle, 2003; Stephenson, 2002). It is perhaps obvious that outcomes of a short-term program would likely be different from a long-term one, but it is very much more difficult to account for these differences in outcomes research due to the extreme variety in experiences. Much of the quantitative outcomes literature takes a very positivistic view of study abroad: it is a static, homogeneous experience. It does not consider study abroad as a dynamic experience in which the outcome is a product of the unique individual interactions with the program and host culture. Even much of the qualitative research is based on interviews with students post-sojourn and therefore is not able to capture the dynamics of the experience itself and how the experience may influence student engagement with the host culture and thus outcomes. There is a small body of such research that is considered in the next chapter on critical perspectives on study abroad.

Summary

Despite a growing emphasis on postsecondary study abroad participation in response to the increasing realities of living and working in a "new global century"

(AAC&U, 2007; APLU, 2004; Green, Luu, and Burris, 2008; NAFSA, 2003), international education advocates have yet to fully demonstrate that participating in a study abroad program will improve intercultural competence (Vande Berg, 2007). The same can be said for a host of other outcomes. As this review suggests, the challenge is highlighted by the lack of theoretically grounded, methodologically rigorous research on the effects of study abroad participation that fully accounts for the array of potentially confounding factors. This includes a pretest/posttest data collection, a large sample gathered from a range of institutional types, data accounting for a wide array of precollege characteristics, educational interests and attitudes, college experiences, and a conceptual model grounded in an empirically vetted theoretical framework addressing the impact of college and college experiences on student development. By no means are we suggesting that the identified problems invalidate the existing research. Methodological weaknesses aside, it is clear that study abroad has more positive than negative outcomes even if these positive gains are not as great as presumed or portrayed. However, understanding the shortcomings of the research on study abroad is critical to the extent that the research informs national and institutional policy.

Study Abroad: Critical Perspectives

B ELIEFS IN THE INHERENT GOODNESS of study abroad are so
strongly interwoven into the narrative of U.S. higher education that study
abroad is rarely critically examined. In fact, Zemach-Bersin (2007) describes
a campaign in support of study abroad extending from the federal government
to institutions that resembles a missionary crusade of sorts. Although they may
take a critical and questioning stance to their own work, rarely do faculty, policymakers, study abroad directors or advocates question study abroad, its purposes, or its benefits. We argue that it is essential to examine the critical
perspectives in order for study abroad to fulfill the high expectations set for it.
The critiques that do exist tend to fall into one of several categories:

- Critiques of the implicit purposes of study abroad, in particular criticisms
  of study abroad as a political tool or as an instrument of cultural and economic imperialism.
- Critiques of the exclusivity of study abroad programs in serving primarily
  wealthy white students from elite colleges.
- Critiques of the nature of the study abroad experience itself.

In this section we focus primarily on critiques of the purposes and nature
of the experience as we deal with the second critique in the chapter on who
studies abroad.

Critiques of the Unstated Purposes of Study Abroad

Most advocates for study abroad argue that it serves to create interculturally competent citizens who are more sensitive to cultural differences, who speak more than one language, and who are more in tune with their own culture and its strengths and weaknesses. Rarely is study abroad described as an instrument of U.S. economic or diplomatic policy or a tool of U.S. imperialism, and certainly no study abroad program emphasizes these purposes. However, given the history of international exchange and study abroad, it is not surprising that such purposes—and such critiques—have existed. In the interwar period, it was the federal government, through IIE, CIEE, and Fulbright that promoted educational and cultural exchange (Bu, 1999). Bu cites former Assistant Secretary of State for Education and Cultural Affairs Philip Coombs as describing educational exchange as "an irrevocable component of American foreign policy" in the interwar period, the "fourth dimension" or cultural component of a holistic diplomatic approach (p. 397). During the Cold War, international exchange programs sponsored by IIE, Fulbright, and Ford were particularly susceptible to these objectives and criticisms. As Bu notes, educational exchange in this period suffered from competing and conflicting purposes. While the government had political goals in mind when fostering and encouraging educational exchange, educators had different goals and at certain points even criticized the government for using educational programs as instruments of propaganda. However, she also argues that efforts to separate educational from political goals were not very effective. The threat of communism helped to mute serious attacks on international exchange efforts and to the extent that faculty and university international efforts depend on external funding, faculty seemed to be willing participants.

More recently the theme of this genre of critique is that study abroad is both an example and instrument of commercialism and the consumer mentality that has come to characterize all of higher education. Bolen (2001) observes that "federal aid, government policy, and study abroad advocates have joined together in the past decade [1980s and 1990s] to create a mass market for American exchange programs" (p. 185). In particular he bemoans the growth in prepackaged consumer experiences. He likens many study abroad programs to tourist experiences: "Participants buy the program to experience the full flavor of the country they study" (p. 186). This consumer identity mentality meshes with the need to consume others' cultures for the instrumental purpose of helping U.S. students get jobs. In fact, the rationale for study abroad frequently emphasizes its role in promoting individual and national success in a global economy. To this end, Zemach-Bersin (2009) concludes that advertising mechanisms portray study abroad as adventure, a means to personal advancement, and cross-cultural understanding, all of which can be bought in nice neat little packages. As Bolen (2001) says, "Bluntly put, Americans need international programs to compete better in the marketplace" (p. 187). In his view, commercialization is inevitable, increasing the pressure on institutions to justify the academic seriousness of study abroad while creating appealingly packaged tourist cultural experiences. Bolen seems not to be so much against this trend as he recognizes the multiple pressures faced by institutions and study abroad programs to have stable, if not growing, enrollments, including more diverse students.

A more severe criticism of study abroad is that it is merely another form of colonialism (Zemach-Bersin, 2007) and that study abroad participants are new colonials (Ogden, 2007/2008). Zemach-Bersin (2007) argues that "proponents of international education identify study abroad as a remedy for widespread cross-cultural misunderstanding, prejudice, global ignorance, and failed international policy" (p. 17). She goes on to say that "such enthusiasm, however, overlooks the many ways in which the discourse of study abroad surreptitiously reproduces the logic of colonialism, legitimizes American imperialist desires, and allows for the interests of U.S. foreign policy to be articulated through the specious rhetoric of global universality" (p. 17). Reviewing a host of recent government-sponsored documents, she finds that amid an "appealing veneer of multicultural understanding and progressive global responsibility, the current discourse of study abroad is nationalistic, imperialist, and political in nature" (p. 17). By implication, institutions offering study abroad are willing partners "eagerly 'internationalizing' their campuses by increasing the accessibility and variety of study abroad programs for their students" (Zemach-Bersin, 2007, p. 18). This is not an entirely new critique. Bu entitled her 2003 study of educational exchange in the twentieth century *Making the World Like Us.* One need not even read the book to get the point.

In a subsequent qualitative study, Zemach-Bersin (2009) studied how study abroad advertising messages affect students' understanding of study abroad. She finds that institutional documents use a "depoliticized rhetoric of 'global citizenship'" (p. 18). She particularly problematizes the concept of *global citizenship* and argues that the term is constructed by those in power while portraying the world as passive and open to *discovery* and *exploration* (terms that appear in advertising). She argues that the United States has engaged in an imperialistic act of creating a status of global citizenship and the process for gaining it—through attaining global competencies and all of the outcomes identified above. This kind of citizenship, she argues, is conferred by institutions of higher education and is granted to those who study abroad but not to those who do not. From this perspective, global citizenship is not universal. Rather, it is exclusive to those who have access to "elitist modes of attaining citizenship" (p. 22).

In short, Zermach-Bersin (2007) argues that by conferring the right to travel, study abroad is merely an upper class means of imperialism in which profits return to the "mother country." She argues that U.S. students studying abroad "extract resources" to be used for their advantage (career preparation) and to the advantage of U.S. economy. Students become "unassuming ambassadors, veiled and covert champions of American diplomacy" (p. 24). In support of her claim, she quotes the editor of the *Journal of the New England Board of Higher Education* as touting study abroad as a good way to "spread democracy around the world . . . and boost America's economic competitiveness at the same time" (p. 25). She sees study abroad professionals as somewhat innocent appropriators of such heroic terms as *global citizenship* and *global understanding* to advance what she sees as U.S. imperialistic efforts. In the end, she argues that the way in which study abroad is promoted undermines the very goals it seeks to promote.

In their book, *Rockin' in Red Square: Critical Approaches to International Education in the Age of Cyberspace,* Grünzweig and Rinehart (2002) gather a number of critical essays on international education. Two chapters in particular, one by Engle and Engle and another by Citron, provide interesting and thought-provoking critiques of the meaning of study abroad in a global age. Both highlight an irony of study abroad in an age of globalization: study abroad is necessary in a globalized world to foster intercultural learning, cross-cultural deepening, and global competence, but as the world becomes globalized, it actually may be more difficult to achieve those learning outcomes. The point is that the value of study abroad is premised on the idea of sending students to the unfamiliar. In fact, study abroad in other English-speaking countries is often not viewed as challenging at all (Ashley, 2011). However, the Internet, CNN, ATMs, and other trappings of a globalized world make finding the unfamiliar difficult even in non-English-speaking countries. Consequently, students cannot be expected to achieve deep cultural understanding just by going abroad. Although study abroad experts are beginning to recognize this fact about all study abroad, Citron (2002) and Engle and Engle (2002) suggest that the extent of globalization makes specific, structured intervention essential to learning. Without sustained and structured onsite activities, deep cultural learning is not likely to occur. In fact, the commercialized nature of education and of study abroad exerts pressure to provide pleasurable experiences that rarely "stiffly challenge participants to examine their attitudes and behavior, and open themselves to the different" in doing so "we often simply aid in the creation of the student parallel world" (Engle and Engle, 2002, p. 34). Engle and Engle recommend better, not more, study abroad options, while Anderson (2003) recommends more of what she calls interpretive interventions (taking advantage of teachable moments) while onsite to encourage deeper learning. Engle and Engle's critique must be seen in light of the fact that they seem to prefer the much more traditional immersion experience to the plethora of study abroad types existing today. To add even more complexity to the situation, Ashley (2011) suggests that study abroad in native-English-speaking countries provides adjustment challenges, often overlooked, that requiring structured learning and interventions.

Gore (2005, 2009) takes a somewhat different approach, arguing that the policy discourse about study abroad reflects "... a constellation of dominant beliefs has coalesced to form an episteme held by the U.S. higher education community: an episteme that defines study abroad as academically weak and without significant functional purpose, a prevailing definition that has marginalized study abroad in the U.S. academic community for decades" (p. 24). Moreover, she finds that study abroad is cast as an activity for women: "Dominant discourse suggests that study abroad programs are perceived as attracting wealthy women to academically weak European programs established in a frivolous Grand Tour tradition" (p. 24) disconnected from preparation for work. She argues that there are plenty of alternative discourses, for example, faculty members who plan serious, rigorous programs that are ignored—by whom, she is not clear. While uncovering the discourse is critical to change, Gore proposes rigorous research on study abroad as a counterdiscourse. Of course, research as discourse has its own set of embedded values and assumptions.

Critical Studies of the Study Abroad Experience

Another strand of research, typically based on qualitative studies of the study abroad experience *in situ,* end up being, perhaps unintentionally, somewhat critical of some aspect of the experience from the students' view. For example, Twombly's (1995) and Anderson's (2003) studies of the role of gender in the experiences of students in study abroad programs in Costa Rica, Talburt and Stewart's (1999) study of a summer Spanish course in Spain, and Wilkinson's (1998a, 1998b, 2000) studies of the immersion experience in France challenge the notion that study abroad is always a positive experience for women or racial and ethnic minorities. Polanyi (1995) argues that harassment negatively affected female students' achievement in Russian oral proficiency. Other studies from the participants' point of view suggest outcomes that are neither intended nor desired (or even imagined) by program organizers (for example, Citron, 2002; Zemach-Bersin, 2009).

Female study abroad students in Costa Rica had trouble making friends and dealing with some aspects of the cultural practices regarding women (responding to unwanted verbal harassment called *piropos*) (Anderson, 2003; Twombly, 1995). These challenges discouraged students who were optimistic about their goals of becoming fluent Spanish speakers and for learning about the culture. Women in both studies believed that difficulties making friends limited their learning. To combat the constant "piropoing," female students reported that they often wore headphones to block the external interference.

Unfortunately, in so doing, they also blocked out the local culture as well (Twombly, 1995). Talburt and Stewart (1999) studied both the in and out of class learning about culture in a five-week study abroad program in Spain. These authors argue that student experiences are filtered through race and gender in ways that have a negative impact on students' overall experiences.

Wilkinson's (1998a, 1998b) study of a French summer study abroad experience challenged several popular beliefs about study abroad. She argues that increased out-of-class interaction with the host culture is not automatic: linguistic improvement is not guaranteed, nor is cultural understanding, "particularly if participants have only their own cultural perspective with which to make sense of actions motivated by an alternative and invisible set of rules" (p. 33). Furthermore, Wilkinson's study showed, as did Twombly's (1995), the varying benefits and faults of the host family, typically viewed as the gold-standard housing arrangement. Moreover, Wilkinson argues that when students' experiences do not conform to the ideal, we ought not necessarily blame the students for being lazy.

Citron (2002) describes students in a study abroad program in Spain as forming a "third culture" that was neither Spanish nor completely North-American. Although Citron's students engaged in U.S.-style approaches to things like grades and hanging out at U.S.-style bars, their lives were not totally as they would be in the United States. Citron explains "third culture" formation as a complex relationship between "context factors, program factors, and group factors" and individual goals, language skills, financial resources, and other personality traits (p. 48). He recognizes that while some of these factors are out of program directors' control, others are not. For example, discouraging e-mail contact with home and having visitors from home while providing more direct orientation or cultural interpreters can enhance contact with the host culture.

Nearly all of the qualitative studies discussed so far have identified some version of this "third culture." The question that remains is whether this "third culture" is inevitable and whether it is in and of itself a negative as usually portrayed. Although not specifically addressing the "third culture," Anderson's (2003) research suggests that study abroad directors and researchers are beginning to recognize that hanging around with other North Americans may have benefits, such as providing safety in numbers for female study abroad participants and buffering students from information overload in early stages of their sojourn (Wilkinson, 1998a, 1998b). Souders (2006) proposes that American students' relations with other North American study abroad participants have an impact on their identity formation. Citron (2002) acknowledges that student who stayed longer exhibited fewer "third culture" characteristics.

In a more recent study, Zemach-Bersin (2009) interviewed twenty-five Wesleyan University students who studied abroad. Her main purpose was to learn how various advertising messages affected students' understanding of the study abroad experience. The results provide a clear example of the gap between the rhetoric of study abroad purposes and outcomes and students' experiences. Most of the Wesleyan students had not consciously thought about studying abroad or where they would go. They tended to see it as an entitlement, which may be due to the demographic characteristics of Wesleyan students, which oddly, given the critical nature to her writing, Zemach-Bersin does not seem to problematize. Their reasons for doing study abroad were mostly to take a break and get out of town, a finding supported by Lucas (2009). Students shopped for study abroad the way they would buy something from L. L. Bean, by looking through catalogs or websites. They knew little about their intended destinations and did not take orientation seriously. Twombly (1995) found a similar reaction in her study of students in Costa Rica. They knew where they were going, but they did little to study up on the country, claiming they didn't want to be tainted by someone else's views of the country. One of the positive outcomes Zemach-Bersin noted was that Wesleyan students came to problematize the concept of global citizenship. Some recognized the lack of clear meaning while others disagreed that they had become global citizens. Still others said that it was unethical for institutions to claim global citizenship as an outcome.

Authors of these various studies are not arguing against study abroad. Rather they all argue that study abroad coordinators could and should do more to turn challenging situations into positive learning experiences for students. This is not as easy or straightforward as it seems. Problematizing the experience of study abroad by raising questions about race, class, and gender or the concept of global citizenship comes into direct conflict with the need to package, present, and sell study abroad as a positive, life-changing adventure of discovery that will lead to intercultural competence and to positive career outcomes. For example, given that women remain the majority of study abroad participants, the fact that women may experience problems and difficulties in the study abroad site is not exactly what study abroad organizers want to advertise (Twombly, 1995).

Despite the critiques, Hoffa (2002) cautions that in our quest to achieve ambitious learning goals, we ought not impose our traditional views of study abroad outcomes on students of today. He argues that students are typically satisfied with their experiences and are aware that they are not in the United States.

Summary

Critical perspectives on study abroad suggest that in order to maximize the potential of study abroad, and to not promote activities directly in conflict with its goals, we ought to thoughtfully consider its rationale and the ways in which we promote study abroad. This includes a careful consideration of the meaning of globalization for study abroad. Additionally, the limited qualitative research on study abroad as actually experienced suggests that much more of this kind of research is necessary if we are to fully understand the outcomes of study abroad and ways in which the experience itself can be improved to enhance student learning.

Conclusions, Final Thoughts, and Recommendations

A S THE PRECEDING REVIEW has shown, study abroad has a long and venerable history in U.S. higher education. Over the course of the twentieth and twenty-first centuries, study abroad has grown from a small initiative for a relatively few well-off white women who spent their junior years abroad to a huge enterprise enrolling more than a quarter million U.S. college students yearly in a range of programs and locations that almost boggles the mind. The purposes and shape of study abroad have changed and broadened in response to global, national, higher education, and institutional trends and pressures. And yet, despite widespread urging by the major higher education policy organizations, politicians, employers, and educators, and the availability of programs to suit almost any interest and need, a very small percentage of the total number of postsecondary students ever studies abroad.

Policymakers and educators alike have set very high goals for study abroad: to produce graduates who are interculturally competent to function in a global economy. A review of the research on a wide range of outcomes, including intercultural competence, suggests that study abroad does result in positive outcomes. For example, participants do seem to graduate on time and at higher rates than those who do not study abroad. Participants are more open- and global-minded and their language skills improve; they are more serious about their studies, more reflective about their own American identity, and more critical of the United States and its role in the world, among other positive outcomes.

Despite all of these positives, our review also suggests that the outcomes may not be as overwhelmingly clear or positive as educators want to believe or as warranted by the investment. That is, when carefully designed studies are able to consider the many variables that may have an effect on study abroad outcomes, those outcomes seem almost underwhelming relative to the hope and hype. Too often, we are left with the nagging conclusion that study abroad results in benefits because the students who participate would have displayed at least some of the outcomes whether or not they had engaged in formal study abroad experiences.

Anyone who has traveled abroad for any length of time recognizes the benefits of traveling and the effects it has on a host of attitudes and skills. The question is: What unique contributions does study abroad make to student learning and development independent of differences in individual characteristics and experiences? A corollary question may be whether study abroad is the best, most cost-effective means of achieving some of the goals society and higher educational leaders have for it, especially in light of the reality that study abroad will likely remain an option for a relatively small percentage of college students. As it turns out, the research on study abroad—and thus this monograph—is not able to provide clear, definitive answers to these questions. At least, we conclude that the strength of outcomes are varied enough to question whether study abroad is achieving the lofty goals set for it by the Lincoln Commission, AAC&U or institutions themselves. Our synthesis may best be seen as a platform for suggesting ways that institutions can identify what contributions study abroad seeks to make and how colleges and universities can work to ensure that those learning outcomes are achieved.

In this final chapter, rather than rehashing recommendations found in much of the recent research on study abroad, we use the knowledge gained from our review to pose some timely questions about what the literature suggests is a gap or a disconnect between the hopes and promises of study abroad and the actual outcomes. We then propose one approach to closing the gap.

Who Participates, Who Does Not, Why, and What to Do About It?

Much attention has been directed at the issue of how to broaden as well as extend participation in study abroad. The Lincoln Commission set very ambitious goals for the number of students studying abroad, and while some progress toward that goal has been achieved, progress has been too slow. As the data show, women continue to significantly outnumber male participants. Likewise, members of underrepresented student populations are much less likely to participate than white students. There have been some shifts in majors represented in study abroad but STEM majors remain among the least likely to study abroad despite the fact that science is today a truly international field.

From the vast research on this topic we know that barriers for underrepresented student groups include various reasons associated with human, cultural and social capital: cost, lack of information, lack of role models, concerns of family, not viewing study abroad as worth the cost in terms of time or money, and the way in which study abroad is marketed. Financial aid and scholarships certainly help defray costs for those students for whom cost is an obstacle; however, the persistence of low rates among men, low-income, and racial and ethnic minority students suggests that overcoming the cost issue alone is insufficient to increase study abroad participation among these groups. For men, the reasons tend to center around social connections at home, failure of study abroad programs to match their interests, assessment that study abroad is not worth the payoff, and subtle and not-so-subtle messaging that study abroad is for women. The main obstacle to increasing STEM participation appears to be disciplinary and institutional structural barriers that make it difficult for students to meet program requirements and graduate in a timely manner.

Much of the literature recommends better and broader marketing to reach groups currently underrepresented in study abroad. Although we certainly agree that better, more sensitive marketing is needed, we argue that sincere efforts to promote study abroad among the underrepresented populations needs to respond to some of the other concerns expressed, such as what is the payoff, is study abroad worth the investment, and so on. We return to this theme below. There are also institutional barriers that must be considered but are rarely discussed in the literature. These include institutional policies around which credits earned abroad can be used toward a degree, inability to guarantee ahead of time that study abroad courses will count toward a degree requirement, and institutional financial aid policies (Cressey and Stubbs, 2010). We also argue that limiting the institutional definition of study abroad to credit-bearing experiences may limit study abroad participation. Although we agree that it would be nigh on impossible to accurately count study abroad participation if non-credit-bearing experiences were allowed, such experiences as student research, service learning, and working abroad may actually provide many of the same outcomes as formal study abroad. As such, they ought not be discounted.

Outcomes: The Good, the Bad, and the Indifferent

Accurately identifying the unique student learning outcomes from study abroad is a monumental task. As we discussed earlier much of the research on study abroad outcomes suffers from significant methodological limitations. When research can isolate the effects of study abroad independent of input variables and/or can compare equivalent groups of students who study abroad with those who do not, we often cannot control for complexity of program differences much less individual variations in how students experience the sojourn. In fact, compared to the amount of research on study abroad outcomes, there has been very little on the actual experience abroad to help us contextualize outcomes. Finally, and importantly, the beliefs about the positive effects are so deeply ingrained in our higher education narrative that even lukewarm results are interpreted and repeated over and over again taking on fairy tale status. The landmark Carlson, Burn, Useem, and Yachimovicz (1990) study is a perfect example of this. Despite the methodological flaws in the study and the study's modest findings, it is constantly used as evidence that study abroad makes a difference.

These limitations aside, the research generally shows that study abroad is at worst a neutral experience with few gains, such as intellectual development (McKeown, 2009) and at best produces significant gains. For example, study abroad participation does not delay graduation and may even encourage graduation in a timely manner. Students who study abroad show language gains, understand themselves and what it means to be American, are more open-minded, are more global-minded, and are more inclined to engage in diverse experiences. Studies of study abroad alumni suggest that participants attribute their career choices and later life attitudes to some extent to study abroad.

This brings us to the goal of intercultural competence so highly promoted by higher education organizations and the government. Although studies show that study abroad students do make progress on various components of intercultural competence, when the effects of study abroad on intercultural competence, as an integrated competence, are investigated, the results are less convincingly positive. If this finding holds up to further scrutiny, what are study abroad advocates to do? Certainly, reducing study abroad options is neither a likely or good option. We reframe the question by asking whether study abroad can and ought to be expected to meet the goals set for it. That is, can study abroad be the transformational experience we expect it to be, transforming the American college student into a globally oriented, interculturally competent citizen able to compete in a global economy? What would need to change in the way we approach study abroad and/or the experience itself in order for study abroad to meet the goals set for it?

Meeting the Challenge

Based on our review of the study abroad landscape—its historical context, its current state, and the research on patterns of participation and outcomes—it seems that the continued emphasis on participation, under the assumption that deep, sustained learning is somehow automatic or inevitable, may actually have made the likelihood of a meaningful educational impact less predictable and therefore less certain. Moreover, the pressures to drive participation rates upward may well be in part contributing to a widening gap between the growing diversity in higher education generally and the stubbornly consistent homogeneity in study abroad participation.

In light of these observations, to renew, reinforce, and in many ways, return study abroad to its educational origins while situating that purpose in a new century and the substantially broader set of educational outcomes necessary to prepare students and communities to thrive in a globally interconnected society, the focus needs to shift from perpetually increased participation to purposeful educational impact. For study abroad to realize—or even be positioned to realize—the educational expectations long held for it by international educators, higher education institutions, and educational policymakers, we propose the following changes, followed by a consideration of the implications of our proposed changes.

Explicitly design and deliver every study abroad program around precisely determined and clearly articulated educational outcomes

These outcomes can, and should, range from discipline-specific content knowledge to professional competencies to complex cognitive skills and outcomes as required by each individual study abroad program's educational goals, curricular or cocurricular function, unique opportunities, and realistic limitations. Most importantly, the specific outcomes selected for any study abroad program need to be plausible and achievable. This means that, no matter whether the program is designed by an institution's own faculty or offered by a third-party provider, every study abroad program must have specific educational expectations that are publicly articulated and assessed. No matter the locus of control or proportion of institutional control over instructor selection, course design, or pedagogical approach, the institution is not absolved from determining whether or not a given study abroad program is providing a minimum threshold of educational contribution toward the institution's overall educational outcomes.

To the degree that an institution offers study abroad programs directed by their own faculty as well as third party providers, the means of making these improvements, while different, are no less achievable. For institutionally sponsored individual study abroad programs, an explicit alignment (or recalibration) of the relationship between the experience and specific educational outcomes involves one or more of a series of initiatives—a closer examination of the program's intended outcomes, its overall design, the pedagogical approach, and the other specific elements of the experience—that can be accomplished by individual program leaders with the support of on-campus resources such as a center for teaching and learning, an office of learning assessment, and potentially the office of student affairs.

To ensure the educational quality of third-party provider programs, higher education institutions have the luxury of relying on free-market mechanisms to drive educational improvement. If institutions establish educational design and learning assessment thresholds for third-party programs that rise to the level of many of the financial and study safety protocols that most institutions already require, third-party providers would be forced to respond to them or face a severe drop in participation and revenue. The Forum on Education Abroad has already developed a robust set of standards called Standards of Good Practices for Education Abroad (2011). This document provides an excellent example of a series of questions—they call them "Queries" (pp. 13–14)—that can function in such a capacity for an institution intent on ensuring that the wide range of the third-party study abroad programs it contracts maintains ideal conditions for learning. For that matter, a thorough embrace of this document would move an institution a long way toward ensuring that all of the study abroad programs it supports delivers a legitimate measure of educational quality.

A focus on intentional learning outcomes may also have the benefit of encouraging program organizers and sponsors to think more carefully about what it means to be a globally competent citizen and the problematic connotations such terms can have.

Don't assume that studying abroad improves intercultural competence

Educators and policymakers need to decouple study abroad from the almost knee-jerk expectation that an international experience necessarily produces or increases cross-cultural awareness, sensitivity, understanding, or intercultural competence. We are in no way trying to suggest that these outcomes are not a reasonable outgrowth of a given study abroad program—but this would only be so to the degree that such a program was explicitly designed to impact student growth on such outcomes. For example, a program that spends a semester immersed in the midst of a bustling cultural center like Mumbai or Shanghai might be ideally suited to develop intercultural competence, whereas a four-week archeology course sequestered at a remote Viking or Inca dig site might offer little opportunity for extensive cross-cultural interactions and therefore have little basis for a realistic expectation of increased intercultural competence. We are not alone in expressing this concern. A number of researchers whose work we have cited have made this or a similar point (for example, Anderson 2003; Citron 2002; Engle and Engle, 2002, 2003; Freed, 1995, 1998).

Decoupling study abroad from the obligation to produce intercultural competence is important to consider at both the micro level of individual programs and the macro level of the institution. Higher education institutions muddy the waters considerably when mission statements, strategic planning initiatives, and promotional materials implicitly or explicitly saddle study abroad with the lion's share of the responsibility for global citizenship outcomes. At the very least, the public implications of this assertion make it exceedingly difficult for study abroad professionals to honestly consider authentically aligning study abroad programs with the most appropriate and best-suited educational outcomes.

Utilize a developmental model of learning to accurately align study abroad programs with appropriate and achievable educational outcomes

When institutions suggest that students will develop intercultural competence or global citizenship skills through study abroad, the institution vastly overstates the potential of a study abroad program, by itself, to produce substantive gains on a complex educational outcome that we know takes years to develop. Rather than assigning study abroad with such a herculean (and likely impossible) task, the educational outcomes expected of a study abroad program should reflect the specific aspects of learning that the program is ideally designed to instill. Two well-known and potentially useful models for institutions to utilize to guide outcome selection might be Bloom's Taxonomy of Cognitive Development or Chickering's Psychosocial Theory of Student Development.

For example, many study abroad programs are uniquely able to provide an opportunity to interact across cultural, racial, and ethnic differences. In this instance, the educational outcome of the study abroad program might be a deeper ability to compare and contrast the ways in which cultural differences impact the values of a community in the United States and in the study abroad location. This outcome is attainable within the confines of the study abroad program. By contrast, intercultural competence would be the result of a sequence of experiences that are designed to build off of one another in a cumulative and iterative way. Over the course of that sequence of experiences—a period that would likely take several years—the student develops the depth of knowledge, understanding, aptitudes, skills, and competencies that might lead to measurable improvements in intercultural competence.

Reconceptualize study abroad as an integrated part of an educational sequence of student experiences rather than an independent entity

Study abroad does not exist independently—it is, and always was, intended to function within the broader educational intentions of an undergraduate education. As such, study abroad should fit into the college or university's overall conception of student learning and development. This means that the experiences in which students engage before and after studying abroad cannot be ignored, minimized, or left to chance. Reconceptualizing study abroad suggests extending Brewer and Cunningham's (2009) work on integrating study abroad into individual courses to a broader level. Based on our findings, these experiences may well be vital to attaining the educational outcomes intended of study abroad. In fact, if study abroad functions as a "disequilibriating" experience (borrowing from the language of Piaget to describe experiences that challenge or disrupt one's current paradigm for understanding), then the degree to which institutions ignore intentionally designed post-study abroad learning experiences is the degree to which they fail to ensure the educational benefit of study abroad. Furthermore, as study abroad programs are increasingly offered to students before or after the junior year, programs and institutions need to apply appropriate developmental models of student growth and focus on educational outcomes that match the development stage of the students for which the program is intended.

Reconsidering study abroad as part of a larger sequence presents a wide range of possibilities in constructing an educational experience (a cocurriculum perhaps) that more effectively delivers on complex outcomes such as intercultural competence. It does not seem beyond the realm of possibility that a study abroad program preceded by other experiential pedagogies such as a service-learning course followed by a guided capstone research project might increase both the overall gains on an outcome such as intercultural competence while at the same time increasing the relative educational impact of the study abroad experience itself. While the work of Brewer and Cunningham (2009) reflects similar recommendations, we would be remiss to minimize the potentially critical role that student affairs programming could play toward these educational goals (Engberg, 2007).

Reframe the way institutions assess the educational impact of study abroad

If study abroad is precisely and primarily focused on meeting educational outcomes specific to the goals of each program and in the process of meeting the broader educational outcomes of the institution, then the way in which the educational impact of study abroad is assessed needs to reflect this conceptual shift. First, every study abroad program needs to perpetually assess the degree to which students make gains on its intended educational outcomes instead of focusing assessment measures on student satisfaction. Satisfaction surveys don't provide in-depth information on learning. Instead, they provide information to ensure future participation.

Second, study abroad needs to be assessed in the context of its contributing role to the larger educational endeavor. This means that, in addition to narrowing the scope of outcomes expected of study abroad and more precisely assessing those outcomes, institutions should assess the full sequence of experiences designed to develop complex outcomes, such as intercultural competence, together as a single entity. Many have lamented the siloed nature of higher education and the disjointed educational experience that results. We have made the same mistake in the way that we conceive of study abroad to the detriment of student learning.

Third, the conceptual approach to assessing study abroad within this broader educational endeavor needs to be primarily about improvement rather than a limited focus on evaluation (the approach often engendered by a focus on satisfaction). Because we still have so much more to learn about designing and delivering an optimal educational impact through study abroad given the wide range of program designs available and the growing diversity of student participants, the field needs extensive data that will help it identify and make those improvements, gathered in a climate that values and celebrates the process that leads to improvement. If the ultimate goal of study abroad assessment devolves into the fleeting value of a "thumbs up" or "thumbs down" from senior administrators—especially in the face of shrinking institutional resources and growing external pressures—higher education will create conditions in which study abroad has little incentive or room to engage in the incremental processes that can lead to substantive improvement.

However, all this talk of assessment does not suggest, and should not be interpreted to imply a hyper-quantified approach. On the contrary, there are a host of meaningful measurement mechanisms—surveys, rubrics, reflective writing, and so on—that are equally appropriate and effective assessment tools. The challenge—as with every assessment endeavor—is the intentional effort to articulate outcomes, design and facilitate experiences that develop students along these outcomes, the construction and implementation of assessment measures that provide data specific to the previously identified outcomes, and finally the thoughtful and prudent use of that data to drive meaningful change.

Reframe the way that we assess study abroad might also include reconsidering whether or not "study abroad" as it is currently defined is in fact the most appropriate unit of analysis

If the focus is on the achievement of predetermined educational outcomes, are there assumptions within the very definition of study abroad (for example, crossing an international border, earning academic credit) that need to be challenged? Currently the range of conditions on which a study abroad program can vary is so vast that many have rightly pointed to the difficulty in accurately measuring the impact of study abroad generally. If study abroad programs were less about the academic ("study") and international ("abroad") components and more about the demonstrable educational outcomes, maybe it would be actually easier to ensure and demonstrate the importance of these experiences as a part of an undergraduate education. This does beg other important questions that shouldn't be ignored. For example, could off-campus study programs that don't cross an international border be just as effective in generating learning gains? Likewise, could some off-campus programs be better suited for the freshman year instead of the traditional junior year?

Change the question by which we judge student participation rates from "how many" to "which ones"

If study abroad is reconceived around intended educational outcomes, then increasing participation is a misdirected end, if not inefficient stewardship of institutional resources. Our review suggests that the students most likely to participate in study abroad are also the students who often already score comparatively high on measures of intercultural competence and language proficiency or have already traveled internationally. Conversely, the students who score comparatively low in intercultural competence or have never traveled internationally are the ones who tend not to study abroad. Thus, instead of prioritizing an ever-increasing number of students who study abroad, the question should be whether or not the students for whom the outcomes of study abroad best fit their educational needs or postgraduate aspirations are actually the ones who represent the majority of participants. In other words, institutions should focus on identifying the students for whom the educational outcomes of a given study abroad program are particularly germane to their educational needs or postgraduate goals. In this context, formal and informal advising practices would explicitly guide students to engage in optional yet educationally valuable experiences such as study abroad that specifically and intentionally lead to the educational and developmental outcomes these students need or hope to achieve. Addressing the "for whom" question also allows us to think about how institutions can develop intercultural competence in those students who will not have a chance to study abroad.

This is not to say that students who have already developed high levels of intercultural competence or have already traveled internationally should be somehow prohibited or discouraged from studying abroad. On the contrary, study abroad should by all means remain an opportunity open to all students. However, an outcomes-based approach recalibrates the purpose of study abroad and, as a result, should reshape the nature of the institutional investment and the marketing messaging of study abroad. An outcomes-based approach to institutional investment in study abroad allows an institution to think less about perpetually increasing the array of locations and program types available and more about investing in the programs that contribute to the educational outcomes of the institution and defraying the costs of the students that would not be able to participate without financial support. Likewise, marketing messages—a subject of particularly pointed criticism (Zemach-Berin, 2009)—can focus now on the link between a study abroad program and the educational outcomes it supports, rather than trying to portray a given program as little more than a fun adventure.

Final Thoughts

We realize that our recommendations challenge the dominant paradigm of study abroad and are not easily achieved. In the current environment it will be a brave study abroad director, academic dean, or university president who puts the brakes on increasing participation numbers and shifts the focus to outcomes. Study abroad directors and those to whom they report will need to become conversant in outcomes language and methodology, and face the even greater challenge of convincing faculty to do the same. Here we also recognize that study abroad administrators are often isolated from faculty and treated as mere support personnel rather than as valuable educational partners. Administrators will need to rethink expectations for growth in study abroad while also working with faculty to identify other curricular and cocurricular means of developing skills such as intercultural competence. Other off-campus experiential learning pedagogies such as service-learning and campus-community partnership projects have demonstrated some overlap with study abroad in achieving important cross-cultural educational outcomes. Moreover, recent developments in international classroom collaborations using online technologies have introduced intriguing possibilities for achieving some of the educational outcomes of cross-cultural interactions at substantially reduced costs. At the same time, we also realize that an overly narrow focus on assessment (to wit, NCLB) could reduce the wonder and spontaneity of the study abroad experience and, if redesigned in a way that prioritizes outcomes, might constrain the potential of new educational benefits that we do not current recognize or understand. That is certainly not our intention.

However, without a shift in focus to outcomes, study abroad will continue to drift along as a predominantly boutique mechanism that works to divide the haves and have-nots in higher education just as much as it might provide some educational opportunity or potential. As Cressey and Stubbs (2009) note, study abroad is expensive (they estimated between \$13,000 and \$23,000 in 2008) and costs of study abroad have increased twice as fast as the consumer price index (Cressey and Stubbs, 2009). Although loans and grants have mitigated the costs somewhat, study abroad remains a very expensive investment for which the expectations are unreasonably high and the outcomes less than astonishing. At the same time, those who cannot or choose not to study abroad will be left without opportunities at home to develop critical intercultural competence outcomes. Refocusing on study abroad outcomes could actually have the added benefit of increasing participation as those groups that currently lag in participation rates may see value in study abroad. Thus, focusing on study abroad outcomes in the ways suggested might actually help higher education, in this one instance, function equally well for all students.

Notes

1. The term *sojourner* is often used in the study abroad literature to describe the individual studying abroad who temporarily resides and studies in a foreign country.
2. See Grünzweig, and Rinehart (2002) for a fuller discussion of globalization in relation to study abroad.
3. See Gore (2005) for an extended analysis of the use and meaning of the Grand Tour in the United States.
4. This section is adapted from Salisbury (2011).
5. The sections on intercultural competence are adapted from Salisbury (2011).
6. Numerous terms are used in the literature for this concept. In recent years a consensus has emerged around the use of the term *intercultural competence*. For a more complete discussion of intercultural competence, see Salisbury (2011).

References

Adelman, C. (1994). *What employers expect of college graduates: International knowledge and second language skills.* (Department of Education publication #OR-94-3215). Washington, DC: U.S. Government Printing Office.

AIFS Abroad (n.d.). Why do institutions work with AIFS? Retrieved November, 2011, from www.aifsabroad.com/advisors/why.asp.

Allen, H. W. (2010). What shapes short-term study abroad experiences? A comparative case study of students' motives and goals [Case study]. *Journal of Studies in International Education, 14,* 452–470. doi: 10.1177/1028315309334739

Allport, G. W. (1954). *The nature of prejudice.* Cambridge, MA: Addison-Wesley.

American Council on Education (ACE). (2002). *Beyond September 11: A comprehensive national policy on international education.* Washington, DC: American Council on Education.

American Council on Education (ACE). (2008). *College-bound students' interests in study abroad and other international learning activities.* Washington, DC: American Council on Education.

Amir, Y. (1969). Contact hypothesis in ethnic relations. *Psychological Bulletin, 71,* 319–342.

Anderson, A. (2003, Fall). Women and cultural learning in Costa Rica: Reading the contexts. *Frontiers: The Interdisciplinary Journal of Study Abroad, 9,* 21–52.

Anderson, P. H., Lawton, L., Rexeisen, R. J., and Hubbard, A. C. (2006). Short-term study abroad and intercultural sensitivity: A pilot study. *International Journal of Intercultural Relations, 30,* 457–469.

Armstrong, G. K. (1984). Life after study abroad: A survey of undergraduate academic and career choices. *Modern Language Journal, 68,* 1–6.

Arum, S. (1987). International education: What is it?: A taxonomy of international education of U.S. universities. *Occasional Papers on International Education.* Retrieved November, 2011, from www.Ciee.org/home/research-publications/papers.aspx.

Ashley, B. (2011). *Challenging assumptions and reconceptualizing frameworks for culturally similar study abroad experiences.* Paper presented at the Association for the Study of Higher Education Annual Conference, Charlotte, NC.

Association of Public and Land-Grant Universities (APLU). (2004). A call to leadership: The presidential role in internationalizing the university. Final report from the Task Force on International Education to the National Association of State Universities and Land Grant Colleges. Retrieved July 12, 2012, from www.aplu.org/NetCommunity/Document.Doc?id=340.

Association of American Colleges and Universities (AAC&U). (2007). College learning for the new global century. A report from the National Leadership Council for Liberal Education & America's Promise. Retrieved from http://www.aacu.org/leap/documents /GlobalCentury_final.pdf.

Astin, A. (1977). Four critical years: Effects of college on beliefs, attitudes, and knowledge. San Francisco: Jossey-Bass.

Barrutia, R. (1971). Study abroad. *Modern Language Journal, 55,* 232–234.

Baxter Magolda, M. (2001). Making their own way: Narratives for transforming higher education to promote self-development. Sterling, VA: Stylus.

Bhandari, R. (2009). Diversification of higher education worldwide: Typologies & definitions in global mobility. Paper presented at the NAFSA, Los Angeles, CA.

Bicknese, G. (1974). Study abroad Part I: A comparative test of attitudes and opinions. *Foreign Language Annals, 7,* 325–336.

Bikson, T. K., and Law, S. A. (1994). *Global preparedness and human resources: College and corporate perspectives.* Santa Monica, CA: RAND Corporation Institute on Education and Training.

Bikson, T. K., Treverton, G. T., Moini, J., and Lindstrom, G. (2003). *New challenges for international leadership: Lessons from organizations with global missions.* Santa Monica, CA: RAND Corporation National Security Research Division.

Biscarra, A. (n.d.). Research and literature on U.S. students study abroad: An update, 2004–2011. Retrieved August 4, 2012, from globaledresearch.com/book_research_comp _update.asp?year=2004.

Black, H. T., and Duhon, D. L. (2006). Assessing the impact of business study abroad programs on cultural awareness and personal development. *Journal of Education for Business, 81*(3), 140–144.

Black, J. S., and Mendenhall, M. (1991). The u-curve adjustment hypothesis revisited: A review and theoretical framework. *Journal of International Business Studies, 22,* 225–247.

Blum, D. E. (2006, October 27). Seeking to prepare global citizens, colleges push more students to study abroad. *Chronicle of Higher Education.* Retrieved June 5, 2012, from http://chronicle.com/article/Seeking-to-Prepare-Global-C/23025/.

Bolen, M. C. (2001). Consumerism and U.S. study abroad. *Journal of Studies in International Education, 5*(3), 182–200. doi: 10.1177/102831530153002

Booker, R. (2001, November). Differences between applicants and non-applicants relevant to the decision to study abroad. Paper presented at the Association for the Study of Higher Education (ASHE) International Forum, Richmond, Virginia.

Borcover, A. (2002, September 8). Travel industry still feeling 9/11. *Chicago Tribune.* Retrieved September 20, 2012, from http://articles.chicagotribune.com/2002-09-08 /travel/0209070124_1_tourism-industry-travel-industry-association-travel-business -roundtable.

Bowman, J. E. (1987). Educating American undergraduates abroad: The development of study abroad programs by American colleges and universities. CIEE Occasional Papers on International Education. Retrieved December 29, 2011, from www.ciee.org/images/uploaded/pdf/occasional24.pdf.

Braskamp, L. A., Braskamp, D. C., and Merrill, K. C. (2009). Assessing progress in global learning and development of students with education abroad experiences. *Frontiers: The Interdisciplinary Journal of Study Abroad, 18,* 101–118.

Brecht, R., Davidson, D., and Ginsberg, R. (1995). *Predicting and measuring language gains in study abroad settings.* In B. F. Freed (Ed.) *Second language acquisition in a study abroad context* (pp. 37–66). Amsterdam/Philadelphia: John Benjamins.

Brewer, E., and Cunningham, K. (2009). *Integrating study abroad into the curriculum.* Sterling, VA: Stylus.

Brint, S. (2011). Focus on the classroom: Movements to reform college teaching and learning, 1980–2008. In J. C. Hermanowicz (Ed.), *The American academic profession: Transformation in contemporary higher education* (pp. 44–91). Baltimore, MD: Johns Hopkins University Press.

Brown, L. M. (2002). Going global. *Black Issues in Higher Education, 19*(6), 28–31.

Brux, J. M., and Fry, B. (2010). Multicultural students in study abroad: Their interests, their issues, and their constraints. *Journal of Studies in International Education, 14*(5), 508–527. doi: 10.1177/1028315309342486

Bu, L. (1999). Educational exchange and cultural diplomacy in the Cold War. *Journal of American Studies, 33*(3), 393–415.

Bu, L. (2003). Making the world like us: Education, cultural expansion, and the American century. Westport, CT: Praeger.

Burr, P. L. (2005, Fall). Building study abroad acceptance among Hispanic students: The value of talking to the Hispanic family. *IIE Networker*, 2005, 36–38.

Calhoon, J. A., Wildcat, D., and Annett, C. (2003). Creating meaningful study abroad programs for American Indian postsecondary students. *Journal of American Indian Education, 42*(1), 46–57.

Cardon, P. W., Marshall, B., and Poddar, A. (2011). Using typologies to interpret study abroad preferences of American business students: Applying a tourism framework to international education. *Journal of Education for Business, 86*(2), 111–118. doi: 10.1080/08832323.2010.482949

Carlson, J., Burn, B., Useem, J., and Yachimovicz, D. (1990). *Study abroad: The experience of American undergraduates.* Westport, CT: Greenwood Press.

Carlson, J. S., and Widaman, K. F. (1988). The effect of study abroad during college on attitudes toward other cultures. *International Journal of Intercultural Relations, 12,* 1–17.

Chieffo, L., and Griffiths, L. (2004). Large-scale assessment of student attitudes after a short-term study abroad program. *Frontiers: The Interdisciplinary Journal of Study Abroad, 10,* 165–177.

Chieffo, L., and Griffiths, L. (2009). Here to stay: Increasing acceptance of short-term study abroad programs. (pp. 365–380). In R. Lewin (Ed.) *The handbook of practice and research in study abroad: Higher education and the quest for global citizenship*. NY: Routledge.

Chmela, H. (2005, October 19). Foreign detour en route to a college degree. *New York Times*. Retrieved October 15, 2011, from http://travel.nytimes.com/2005/10/19/education /19goucher.html?_r=1 &scp=1&sq=%22lincoln+commission%22+and+%22study +abroad%22&st=nyt.

Chow, P. (2010). Brazil-U.S. international educational exchange: Data from the Open Doors Report on International Educational Exchange. PowerPoint presentation. Retrieved September 2012, from http://www.iie.org/en/Research-and-Publications/Publications-and-Reports/IIE-Bookstore/~/media/Files/Corporate/Membership/FAUBAI_2010.ashx.

Church, A. T. (1982). Sojourner adjustment. *Psychological Bulletin, 91,* 540–572.

Churchill, E., and DuFon, M. A. (2006). Evolving threads in study abroad research. In M. A. DuFon and E. Churchill (Eds.), *Language learners in study abroad contexts* (pp. 1–29). Clevedon, England: Multilingual Matters.

Citron, J. L. (2002). U.S. students abroad: Host culture integration or third culture formation? In W. Grünzweig and N. Rinehart (Eds.), *Rockin' in Red Square: Critical approaches to international education in the time of cyberculture* (pp. 41–56). Munster, Germany: Lit Verlag.

Clarke, I., Flaherty, T. B., Wright, N. D., and McMillen, R. M. (2009). Student intercultural proficiency from study abroad programs. *Journal of Marketing Education, 31*(2), 173–181.

Commission on the Abraham Lincoln Study Abroad Fellowship Program. (2005). Global competence and national needs: One million Americans studying abroad. Final Report from the Commission on the Abraham Lincoln Fellowship Program, Washington, DC.

Comp, D. J. (n.d.a). Research and literature on U.S. students abroad 1988–2000. A bibliography with abstracts. Retrieved August 4, 2012, from chicago.academia.edu/DavidComp /Papers/76147/Research_and_Literature_on_U.S._Students_Abroad_A_Bibliography_ with_Abstracts_1988–2000.

Comp, D. J. (n.d.b). Research and Literature on U.S. Students Abroad: A Bibliography with Abstracts 2001–2006. Retrieved August 4, 2012, from chicago.academia.edu/DavidComp /Papers/76149/Research_and_Literature_on_U.S._Students_Abroad_A_Bibliography_ with_Abstracts_2001-2006.

Comp, D. (2008). U.S. Heritage-seeking students discover minority communities in Western Europe. *Journal of Studies in International Education, 12*(1), 29–37.

Consolidated Appropriations Act, 2004, Pub. L. No. 108–199, 118 Stat. 3 (2004).

Cornwell, G., and Stoddard, E. (1999). *Globalizing knowledge: Connecting international and intercultural studies*. Washington, DC: Association of American Colleges and Universities.

Council on International Educational Exchange (CIEE). (1991). *Black students and overseas programs: Broadening the base of participation*. Papers and speeches presented at the 43rd CIEE International Conference on Educational Exchange. New York, NY: Council on International Educational Exchange.

Council on International Educational Exchange (CIEE). (n.d.). "About." Retrieved December, 2011 from www.ciee.org/home/about/about-ciee.aspx.

Cressey, W., and Stubbs, N. (2010). The economics of study abroad. In W. W. Hoffa and S. C. DePaul (Eds.), *A history of U.S. study abroad: 1965–present* (pp. 253–294). Carlisle, PA: Forum on Education Abroad.

Cushner, K., and Karim, A. U. (2004). Study abroad at the university level. In D. Landis, J. M. Bennett, and M. J. Bennett (Eds.), *Handbook of intercultural training* (3rd ed., pp. 289–308). Thousand Oaks, CA: Sage.

Cushner, K., and Mahon, J. (2002). Overseas student teaching: Affecting personal, professional, and global competencies in an age of globalization. *Journal of Studies in International Education, 6,* 44–58.

Deardorff, D. K. (2004). *The identification and assessment of intercultural competence as a student outcome of internationalization at institutions of higher education in the United States* (Doctoral dissertation). Raleigh, NC: North Carolina State University. Retrieved August 8, 2012, from repository.lib.ncsu.edu/ir/handle/1840.16/5733.

Deardorff, D. K. (2006). Identification and assessment of intercultural competence as a student outcome of internationalization. *Journal of Studies in International Education, 10*(3), 241–266.

Deardorff, D. K. (2009). Understanding the challenges of assessing global citizenship. In R. Lewin (Ed.), *The handbook of practice and research in study abroad: Higher education's quest for global citizenship* (pp. 346–364). New York: Routledge.

Deficit Reduction Act of 2005, Pub. L. No. 109–171, 120 Stat. 4 (2005).

Dessoff, A. (2006). Who's not going abroad? *International Educator, 15*(2), 20–27.

DeWinter, U. J., and Rumbley, L. E. (2010). The diversification of education abroad across the curriculum. In W. W. Hoffa and S. C. DePaul (Eds.), *A history of U.S. study abroad: 1965–present* (pp. 55–114). Lancaster, PA: Frontiers: The Interdisciplinary Journal of Study Abroad.

Dolby, N. (2004). Encountering an American self: Study abroad and national identity. *Comparative Education Review, 48*(2), 150–173.

Dolby, N. (2007). Reflections on nation: American undergraduates and education abroad. *Journal of Studies in International Education, 11*(2), 141–156.

Douglas, C., and Jones-Rikkers, C. G. (2001). Study abroad programs and American student worldmindedness: An empirical analysis. *Journal of Teaching in International Business, 13,* 55–66.

Du, F. (2007). Self-authorship as a learning outcome of study abroad: Towards a new approach for examining learning and learning conditions (Doctoral dissertation). University of Minnesota, Minneapolis.

Dwyer. M. M. (2004, Fall). More is better: The impact of study abroad duration. *Frontiers: The Interdisciplinary Journal of Study Abroad, 10,* 151–164.

Engberg, M. E. (2007). Educating the workforce for the 21st century: A cross-disciplinary analysis of the impact of the undergraduate experience on the students' development of a pluralistic orientation. *Research in Higher Education, 48,* 283–317.

Engle, J., and Engle, L. (2002). Neither international nor educative: Study abroad in the time of globalization. In W. Grünzweig and N. Rinehart (Eds.), *Rockin' in Red Square:*

Critical approaches to international education in the time of cyberculture (pp. 25–40). Munster, Germany: Lit Verlag.

Engle, L., and Engle, J. (2003). Study abroad levels: Toward a classification of program types. *Frontiers: The Interdisciplinary Journal of Study Abroad, 9,* 1–20.

Falcetta, F. M. (n.d.). The globalization of community colleges. *Study abroad: A 21st century perspective, II.* Retrieved August 8, 2012, from www.aifsfoundation.org/21century.asp.

Falk, R., and Kanach, N. A. (2000). Globalization and study abroad: An illusion of paradox. *Frontiers: The Interdisciplinary Journal of Study Abroad, 4,* 155–168.

Farrell, E. F. (2007, September 7). Study abroad blossoms into big business. *Chronicle of Higher Education.* Retrieved from http://chronicle.com/article/Study-Abroad-Blossoms-Into-/19935/.

Field, R. (Producer and Director). (2009). *Engaging the world: U.S. global competence in the 21st century.* (DVD). (Available from the American Council on Education, One Dupont Circle NW, Washington DC, 20036). Retrieved from www.usglobalcompetence.org /videos/download.html.

Fischer, K. (2007, June 20). All abroad! Overseas study required. *Chronicle of Higher Education.* Retrieved May 14, 2012, from http://chronicle.com/article/All-Abroad-Overseas-Study-/13923/.

Fischer, K. (2012, February 25). In study abroad, men are hard to find. *Chronicle of Higher Education.* Retrieved June 5, 2012, from chronicle.com/article/In-Study-Abroad-Men-Are-Hard/130853.

Flash, S. J. (1999). *Study abroad program participation effects on academic progress* (Doctoral dissertation). State University of New York at Buffalo. Retrieved August 8, 2012, from search.proquest.com/pqdtft/docview/304564726/1386C9B3D2F5B72BF59/1?accountid=14556.

Forum on Education Abroad. (2011) Glossary. January 10, 2012, from www.forumea.org /EducationAbroadGlossary2ndEdition2011.cfm.

Forum on Education Abroad. (n.d.) "About." Retrieved December, 2011, from www.forumea .org/about-mission.cfm.

Freed, B. F. (1995). *Second language acquisition in a study abroad context.* Philadelphia: Benjamins.

Freed, B. F. (1998, Fall). An overview of issues and research in language learning in a study abroad setting. *Frontiers: The interdisciplinary journal of study abroad, 9,* 31–60.

Friedman, T. L. (2005). *The world is flat: A brief history of the twenty-first century.* New York: Farra, Strauss, & Giroux.

Fulbright, J. W. (1989). *The price of empire.* New York: Pantheon.

Fuller, T. L. (2007). Study abroad experiences and intercultural sensitivity among graduate theological students: A preliminary and exploratory investigation. *Christian Higher Education, 6*(4), 321–332.

Gmelch, G. (1997). Crossing cultures: Student travel and personal development. *International Journal of Intercultural Relations, 21,* 475–490.

Golay, P. (2006). *The effects of study abroad on the development of global-mindedness among students enrolled in international programs at Florida State University* (Doctoral dissertation).

Florida State University, Tallahassee. Retrieved August 8, 2012, from search.proquest
.com/pqdtft/docview/305332853/1386C9E15E8147E176D/1?accountid=14556.

Goldstein, S. B., and Kim, R. I. (2006). Predictors of US college students' participation in study abroad programs: A longitudinal study. *International Journal of Intercultural Relations, 30,* 507–521.

Gonyea, R. M. (2008, November). The impact of study abroad on senior year engagement. Paper presented at the Annual Meeting of the Association for the Study of Higher Education, Jacksonville, FL.

Goodman, A. E. (2008). Foreword to expanding study abroad at U.S. community colleges. *IIE study abroad white paper series.* New York: Institute of International Education.

Gore, J. E. (2005). *Dominant beliefs and alternative voices: Discourse, belief, and gender in American study abroad.* New York: Routledge.

Gore, J. E. (2009). Faculty beliefs and institutional values: Identifying and overcoming these obstacles to education abroad growth. In R. Lewin (Ed.), *The handbook of practice and research in study abroad: Higher education and the quest for global citizenship* (pp. 282–302). New York: Routledge.

Green, M. (2005). *Internationalization in U.S. higher education: The student perspective.* Washington, DC: American Council on Education.

Green, M., Luu, D. T., and Burris, B. (2008). *Mapping internationalization on U.S. campuses: 2008 edition.* Washington, DC: American Council on Education.

Grünzweig, W., and Rinehart, N. (Eds.). (2002). *Rockin' in Red Square: Critical approaches to international education in the age of cyberculture.* Munster, Germany: Lit Verlag.

Gullahorn, J. E., and Gullahorn, J. T. (1966). American students abroad: Professional versus personal development. *Annals of the American Academy of Political and Social Science, 368,* 43–59.

Gutierrez, R., Auerbach, J., and Bhandari, R. (2009). Expanding U.S. study abroad capacity: Findings from an IIE-forum survey. In P.B.R. Gutierrez (Ed.), *Expanding study abroad capacity at U.S. colleges and universities.* New York: Institute of International Education.

Hadis, B. F. (2005). Why are they better students when they come back? Determinants of academic focusing gains in the study abroad experience. *Frontiers: The Interdisciplinary Journal of Study Abroad, 11,* 57–70.

Hamir, H. B. (2011). *Go abroad and graduate on-time: Study abroad participation, degree completion, and time-to-degree* (Doctoral dissertation). University of Nebraska, Lincoln. Retrieved April, 2012, from search.proquest.com/pqdtft/docview/864031134/1 386CA12C8C69AF20F1/1?accountid=14556.

He, N., and Chen, R.J.C. (2010). College students' perceptions and attitudes toward the selection of study abroad programs. *International Journal of Hospitality & Tourism, 11,* 347–359. doi: 10.1080/15256480.2010.518525

Heisel, M., and Stableski, R. (2009). Expanding study abroad: Where there's a will, there's a way. In P. B. R. Gutierrez (Ed.), *Expanding study abroad capacity at U.S. colleges and universities.* New York: Institute of International Education.

Hewstone, M., and Brown, R. (1986). Contact is not enough: An intergroup perspective on the "contact hypothesis." In M. Hewstone and R. Brown (Eds.), *Contact and conflict in intergroup encounters* (pp. 1–44). Cambridge, MA: Addison-Wesley.

Hill, B., and Green, M. (2008). *A guide to internationalization for chief academic officers.* Washington, DC: American Council on Education.

Hochhauser, G. A. (2005). Demographic Factors Redefining Education Abroad. *Study Abroad: A 21st century perspective, II.* Retrieved October 4, 2012, from www.aifsfoundation.org /21century.asp.

Hoffa, W. W. (2002). Learning about the future world: International education and the demise of the nation state. In W. Grünzweig and N. Rinehart (Eds.), *Rockin' in Red Square: Critical approaches to international education in the age of cyberculture* (pp. 57–74). Munster, Germany: Lit Verlag.

Hoffa, W. W. (2007). *A history of U.S. study abroad: Beginnings to 1965.* Carlisle, PA: Forum on Education Abroad.

Hoffa, W. W., and DePaul, S. C. (2010). *A history of U.S. study abroad: 1965–present.* Carlisle, PA: Forum on Education Abroad.

IES Abroad. (n.d.). Overview. Retrieved November 2011, from www.iesabroad.org/IES /About_IES/overview.html.

Ingraham, E. C. and Peterson, D. L. (2004). Assessing the impact of study abroad on student learning at Michigan State University. *Frontiers: The interdisciplinary journal of study abroad, 10,* 83–100.

Institute of International Education (IIE). (2009). *Open doors 2009 report on international education exchange: Table 24—profile of U.S. study abroad students, 1998/99–2007/08.* Retrieved from http://opendoors.iienetwork.org/?p=150839.

Institute of International Education (IIE). (2010). *Special reports: Community college data resource.* Retrieved from November, 2011, from www.iie.org/Research-and-Publications /Open-Doors/Data/Special-Reports/Community-College-Data-Resource/Study-Abroad -Characteristics-2008-09.

Institute of International Education (IIE). (2011). *Open doors 20/11 "fast facts."* Retrieved from www.iie.org/en/Research-and-Publications/-/media/Files/Corporate/Open-Doors/Fast-Facts/Fast%20Facts%202011.ashx.

Institute of International Education (IIE) (n.d.a). Leading institutions by institutional type. Retrieved November 11, 2011, from www.iie.org/en/Research-and-Publications/Open-Doors/Data/US-Study-Abroad/Leading-Institutions-by-Institutional-Type/2009-10.

Institute of International Education (IIE). (n.d.b). Student profile. Retrieved November 11, 2011, from www.iie.org/Research-and-Publications/Open-Doors/Data/US-Study-Abroad/Student-Profile/2000-10.

Institute of International Education (IIE). (n.d.c). "History." Retrieved November 11, 2011, from www.iie.org/en/Who-We-Are/History.

Institute of International Education (IIE). (n.d.d). Open Doors data. Retrieved September 19, 2012, from www.iie.org/en/Research-and-Publications/Open-Doors/Data.

Institute of International Education (IIE). (n.d.e). Open Doors, Special Reports: Community College Data Resource. Retrieved October 5, 2012, from www.iie.org/Research-and-Publications/Open-Doors/Data/Special-Reports/Community-College-Data-Resource.

Jackson, M. J. (2005, Fall). Study abroad for students of color: Breaking the barriers to overseas study for students of color and minorities. *IIE Networker*, 16–18.

Jessup-Anger, J. E. (2008). Gender observations and study abroad: How students reconcile cross-cultural differences related to gender. *Journal of College Student Development, 49*(4), 360–373.

Johnston, J. S., Jr., and Edelstein, R. J. (1993). *Beyond borders: Profiles in international education.* Washington, DC: Association of American Colleges and Universities.

Jon, J., and Fry, G. (2009, November 7). The long-term impact of undergraduate study abroad experience: Implications for higher education. Paper presented at the Annual Meeting of the Association for the Study of Higher Education, Vancouver, Canada.

Jorge, E. (2006). A journey home: Connecting Spanish-speaking communities at home and abroad. *Hispania, 89*(1), 110–122.

Jurgens, J. C., and McAuliffe, G. (2004). Short-term study-abroad experience in Ireland: An exercise in cross-cultural counseling. *International Journal for the Advancement of Counseling, 26,* 147–161.

Kalunian, J. (1997, Fall). Correlations between global-mindedness and study abroad. *International Education Forum, 17,* 131–143.

Kasravi, J. (2009). *Factors influencing the decision to study abroad for students of color: Moving beyond the barriers* (Doctoral dissertation). University of Minnesota, Minneapolis.

Kauffmann, N. L. (1983). *The impact of study abroad on personality change* (Doctoral dissertation). Indiana University, Bloomington.

Kegan, R. (1982). *The evolving self: Problems and process in human development.* Cambridge, MA: Harvard University Press.

Kegan, R. (1994). *In over our heads: The mental demands of modern life.* Cambridge, MA: Harvard University Press.

Kim, R. I., and Goldstein, S. B. (2005). Intercultural attitudes predict favorable study abroad expectations of U.S. college students. *Journal of Studies in International Education, 9*(3), 265–278.

Kim, D. B., Twombly, S. B., and Wolf-Wendel, L. (2011). International faculty: Experiences of academic life and productivity in U.S. Universities. *Journal of Higher Education, 82*(6), 720–747.

King, P. M., and Baxter Magolda, M. (1996). A developmental perspective on learning. *Journal of College Student Development, 37,* 163–173.

King, P. M., and Baxter Magolda, M. (2005). A developmental model of intercultural maturity. *Journal of College Student Development, 46,* 571–592.

King, P. M., and Kitchener, K. (1994). *Developing reflective judgment: Understanding and promoting intellectual growth and critical thinking in adolescents and adults.* San Francisco: Jossey-Bass.

King, L. J., and Young, J. A. (1994). Study abroad: Education for the 21st century. *Die Unterrichtspraxis/Teaching German, 27,* 77–87.

Kitsantas, A. (2004). Studying abroad: The role of college students' goals on the development of cross-cultural skills and global understanding. *College Student Journal, 38*(3), 441–452.

Kitsantas, A., and Meyers, J. (2001, March). Studying Abroad. Does it Enhance College Student Cross-Cultural Awareness? Paper presented at combined Annual Meeting of the San Diego State University and the U.S. Department of Education Centers for International Business Education and Research (CIBER 2001), San Diego, CA.

Knight, J. (2004). Internationalization remodeled: Definition, approaches, and rationales. *Journal of Studies in International Education, 8*(5), 5–31. doi: 10.1177/1028315303260832

Koester, J. (1985). *A profile of the U.S. student abroad.* New York: Council on International Educational Exchange.

Kuh, G. D. (2008). *High impact educational practices: What they are, who has access to them, and why they matter.* Washington, DC: Association of American Colleges and Universities.

Lambert, R. D. (1989). *International studies and the undergraduate.* Washington, DC: American Council on Education.

Laubscher, M. R. (1994). *Encounters with difference* (Vol. 105). Westport, CT: Greenwood Press.

Levine, D. O. (1986). *The American college and the culture of aspiration 1915–1940.* Ithaca, NY: Cornell University Press.

Lewin, R. (Ed.). (2009). *The handbook of practice and research in study abroad: Higher education and the quest for global citizenship.* New York: Routledge.

Lindsey, E. W. (2005). Study abroad and values development in social work students. *Journal of Social Work Education, 41,* 229–249.

Lucas, C. J. (2006). *American higher education.* New York: Palgrave Macmillan.

Lucas, J. M. (2009). *Where are all the males? A mixed methods inquiry into male study abroad participation* (Doctoral dissertation). Michigan State University, East Lansing (AAT 3381358). Retrieved April, 2012, from search.proquest.com/pqdtft/docview/304949857 /1386CA4F7684EA8E3BF/1?accountid=14556.

Magnan, S. S., and Back, M. (2007). Social interaction and linguistic gain during study abroad. *Foreign Language Annals, 40,* 43–61.

Malmgren, J., and Galvin, J. (2008). Effects of study abroad participation on student graduation rates: A study of three incoming freshman cohorts at the University of Minnesota, Twin Cities. *NADADA Journal, 28*(1), 29–42.

McClure, K.R.S., Niehaus, E., Anderson, A. A., and Reed, J. (2010). "We just don't have the possibility yet": U.S. Latina/o narratives on study abroad. *Journal of Student Affairs Research and Practice, 47*(3), 367–386. doi: 0.2202/1949-6605.6056

McKeown, J. S. (2003). The impact of September 11 on study abroad student interest and concern: An exploratory study. *International Education, 32*(2), 85–95.

McKeown, J. S. (2009). *The first time effect: The impact of study abroad on college student intellectual development.* Albany: State University of New York Press.

Merva, M. (2003). Grades as incentives: A quantitative assessment with implications for study abroad programs. *Journal of Studies in International Education, 7*(2), 149–156.

Metzger, C. (2006). Study abroad programming: A 21st century retention strategy? *College Student Affairs Journal, 25,* 164–175.

Mikhailova, L. (2002). CIEE History Part I: 1947–1960. Retrieved from www.ciee.org /home/about/documents/history1pdf.

Milstein, T. (2005). Transformation abroad: Sojourning and the perceived enhancement of self-efficacy. *International Journal of Intercultural Relations, 29,* 217–239.

Mistretta, W. (2008). *Life-enhancing: An exploration of the long-term effects of study abroad* (Doctoral dissertation). State University of New York at Buffalo. Retrieved March, 2012, from search.pro-quest.com/pqdtft/docview/304406369/1386CA6C9193856DD4C /4?accountid=14556.

Mount Holyoke College (n.d.). "Study abroad." Retrieved November, 2011, from www.mtholyoke.edu/global/study_abroad.html.

NAFSA: Association of International Educators. (2003). *Securing America's future: Global education for a global age.* Report of the Strategic Task Force on Education Abroad. Retrieved September 23, 2012, from www.nafsa.org/resourcelibrary/default.aspx?id=9115.

NAFSA: Association of International Educators. (2009a). *Lincoln Commission Report.* Retrieved October 4, 2011, from http://www.nafsa.org/resourcelibrary/Default.aspx?id=16035.

NAFSA: Association of International Educators. (2009b). *Foreign Relations Authorization act for Fiscal years 2010 and 2011.* Retrieved October 4, 2011, from http://www.nafsa.org /publicpolicy/default.aspx?id=16130#Simon.

NAFSA: Association of International Educators. (n.d.). "Annual Conference". Retrieved May, 2012, from www.nafsa.org/annualconference/default.aspx?id=16889.

Nash, D. (1976). The personal consequences of a year of study abroad. *Journal of Higher Education, 47,* 191–203.

National Center for Education Statistics (NCES). (2008a). Table A-40-1. Number and percentage distribution of U.S. study abroad students, by host region: Selected academic years, 1987–88 through 2007–08. Retrieved June 10, 2012, from http://nces.ed.gov/ programs/coe/2010/section5/table-ssa-1.asp.

National Center for Education Statistics (NCES). (2008b). Table 189. Total fall enrollment in degree-granting institutions, by attendance status, sex of student, and control of institution: Selected years, 1947 through 2008. Retrieved June 10, 2012, from http://nces.ed.gov /programs/digest/d09/tables/dt09_189.asp.

National Center for Education Statistics (NCES). (n.d.). Enrollment, staff, and degrees conferred in postsecondary institutions. Retrieved January, 2012, from http://nces.ed.gov /programs/digest/d10/tables/dt10_195.asp.

National Commission on Terrorist Attacks Upon the United States. (2003). *The 9/11 commission report.* Washington, DC: U.S. Government Printing Office. Retrieved September 24, 2012, from http://govinfo.library.unt.edu/911/report/911Report.pdf.

National Task Force on Undergraduate Education Abroad. (1990). *A national mandate for education abroad: Getting on with the task.* New York: Council on International Educational Exchange.

Niehaus, E. (2011). *Understanding STEM majors' intent to study abroad.* Paper presented at the NASPA Faculty Fellows Emerging Scholars Research Program Session.

Norris, M. E., and Gillespie, J. (2009). How study abroad shapes global careers: Evidence from the United States. *Journal of Studies in International Education, 13,* 382–397.

Obst, D., Bhandari, R., and Witherell, S. (2007). Meeting America's global challenge: Current trends in U.S. study abroad & the impact of strategic diversity initiatives. *Study abroad white paper series.* New York: Institute of International Education.

Ogden, A. (2007/2008). The view from the veranda: Understanding today's colonial students. *Frontiers: The Interdisciplinary Journal of Study Abroad, 15,* 2–20.

Ogden, A.C., Soneson, H. M., and Weting, P. (2010). The diversification of geographic locations. In W. W. Hoffa and S. C. DePaul (Eds.), *The history of U.S. study abroad: 1965–present* (pp. 161–198). Lancaster, PA: Frontiers Journal Incorporated.

O'Hara, S. (2009). Vital and overlooked: The role of faculty in internationalizing U.S. campuses. *IIE study abroad white paper series.* New York: Institute of International Education.

Olson, C., Green, M., and Hill, B. (2005). *Building a strategic framework for comprehensive internationalization.* Washington, DC: American Council on Education.

Olson, C., Green, M., and Hill, B. (2006). *A handbook for advancing comprehensive internationalization: What institutions can do and what students should learn.* Washington, DC: American Council on Education.

Olson, C. L., and Kroeger, K. R. (2001). Global competency and intercultural sensitivity. *Journal of Studies in International Education, 5*(2), 116–137.

Paige, R. M., and others. (2009). Study abroad for global engagement: The long-term impact of mobility experiences. *Intercultural Education, 20,* 529–544. doi: 10.1080/14675980903370847

Pascarella, E. T. (1985). College environmental influences on learning and cognitive development: A critical review and synthesis. In J. Smart (Ed.). *Higher education: Handbook of theory and research* (Vol. 1, pp. 1–64). New York: Agathon.

Pascarella, E. T., and Terenzini, P. T. (1991). *How college affects students.* San Francisco: Jossey-Bass.

Pascarella, E. T., and Terenzini, P. T. (2005). *How college affects students: Vol. 2. A third decade of research.* San Francisco: Jossey-Bass.

Patterson, P. K. (2006). *Effect of study abroad on intercultural sensitivity* (Doctoral dissertation). University of Missouri-Columbia. Retrieved August 8, 2012, from search.proquest.com/pqdtft/docview/305307788/1386CAAFE2A57F5EFEE/1?accountid=14556.

Paulsen, M. B., and St. John, E. P. (2002). Social class and college costs: Examining the financial nexus between college choice and persistence. *Journal of Higher Education, 73*(2), 189–236. doi: 10.1353/jhe.2002.0023

Paus, E., and Robinson, M. (2008). Increasing study abroad participation: The faculty makes the difference. *Frontiers: The Interdisciplinary Journal of Study Abroad, 17,* 33–49.

Pearson, J. (2005). The role of the institutional setting and its impact on education abroad policy and programs. *Study abroad: A 21st century perspective, II.* Retrieved September 23, 2012, from www.aifsfoundation.org/21century.asp

Pedersen, P. J. (2009). Teaching towards an ethnorelative worldview through psychology study abroad. *Intercultural Education, 20,* 73–86.

Penn, E. B., and Tanner, J. (2009). Black students and international education: An Assessment. *Journal of Black Studies, 40*(2), 266–282. doi: 10.1177/0021934707311128

Perdreau, C. (2003). Building diversity into education abroad programs. *Study abroad: A 21st century perspective.* Retrieved June 10, 2012, from www.aifsfoundation.org/21century.asp.

Perna, L. (2006). Studying college access and choice: A proposed conceptual model. *Higher Education Handbook of Theory and Research* (Vol. 21, pp. 99–157). doi: 10:1007 /1-4020-4512-3_3

Perry, W. (1970). *Forms of intellectual and ethical development in the college years: A scheme.* San Francisco: Jossey-Bass.

Pettigrew, T. F., and Tropp, L. R. (2006). A meta-analytic test of intergroup contact theory. *Journal of Personality and Social Psychology, 90,* 751–783.

Pickard, M. D., and Ganz, M. A. (2005, Fall). Increasing national diversity in education abroad using the Gilman international Scholarship and others. *IIE Networker,* 21–27.

Polanyi, L. (1995). Language learning and living abroad: Stories from the field. In B. F. Freed (Ed.), *Second language acquisition in a study abroad context.* Amsterdam, Netherlands: Benjamins.

Posey, J. T., Jr. (2003). *Study abroad: Educational and employment outcomes of participants and nonparticipants* (Doctoral dissertation). Florida State University. Retrieved October 4, 2012, from search.proquest.com/pqdtft/docview/305325935/1386CAC89984267884/ 1?accountid=14556.

PRWeb. (May 29, 2012). New survey shows college graduates who study abroad land career-related jobs sooner, with higher starting salaries. Retrieved June 1, 2012, from www .prweb.com/releases/2012/5/prweb9541667.htm.

President's Commission on Foreign Languages and International Study. (1980). Strength through wisdom: A critique of U.S. capability. *Modern Language Journal, 64*(1), 9–57.

Presley, A., Damron-Martinez, D., and Zhang, L. (2010). A study of business student choice to study abroad: A test of the theory of planned behavior. *Journal of Teaching in International Business, 21,* 227–247. doi: 10.1080/08975930.2010.526009

Raby, R. L. (2008). Expanding education abroad at U.S. community colleges. *Meeting America's global education challenges: The study abroad white paper series.* New York: Institute for International Education.

Redden, E. (2007a, August 14). Study abroad under scrutiny. *Inside Higher Ed.* Retrieved November, 2012, from www.insidehighered.com/news/2007/08/14/abroad.

Redden, E. (2007b, August 20). The middlemen of study abroad. *Inside Higher Ed.* Retrieved December 29, 2011, from www.insidehighered.com/news/2007/08/20/abroad.

Redden, E. (2008). Women abroad and men at home. *Inside Higher Ed.* Retrieved December 29, 2011, from www.insidehighered.com/news/2008/12/04/genderabroad.

Relyea, C., Cocchiara, F. K., and Studdard, N. L. (2008). The effect of perceived value in the decision to participate in study abroad programs. *Journal of Teaching in International Business, 19*(4), 346–361.

Rodman, R., and Merrill, M. (2010). Unlocking study abroad potential: Design models, methods and masters. In W. W. Hoffa and S. C. DePaul (Eds.), *The history of U.S. study abroad: 1965–present* (pp. 199–252). Lancaster, PA: Frontiers: The Interdisciplinary Journal of Study Abroad.

Rubin, K. (2004). Going to study. *International Educator, 13,* 26–33.

Rust, V., Dhanatya, C., Furuto, L.H.L., and Kheiltash, O. (2007, Fall). Student involvement as predictive of college freshmen plans to study abroad. *Frontiers: The Interdisciplinary Journal of Study Abroad, 15,* 1–16.

Ryan, M., and Twibell, R. (2000). Concerns, values, stress, coping, health, and educational outcomes of college students who studied abroad. *International Journal of Intercultural Relations, 24,* 409–435.

Salisbury, M. H. (2011). *The effect of study abroad on intercultural competence among undergraduate college students* (Doctoral dissertation). University of Iowa, Iowa City. Retrieved November, 2011, from search.proquest.com/pqdtft/docview/879830525 /1386CAD9FD04C036A47/1?accountid=14556.

Salisbury, M., Paulsen, M., and Pascarella, E. (2010). To see the world or stay at home: Applying an integrated student choice model to explore the gender gap in the intent to study abroad. *Research in Higher Education, 51*(7), 615–640. doi: 10.1007/s11162-010-9171-6

Salisbury, M. H., Paulsen, M. B., and Pascarella, E. T. (2011). Why do all the study abroad students look alike? Using an integrated student choice model to explore differences in the development of white and minority students' intent to study abroad. *Research in Higher Education, 52*(2), 123–150. DOI: 10.1007/s11162-010-9191-2

Salisbury, M. H., Umbach, P. D., Paulsen, M. B., and Pascarella, E. T. (2009). Going global: Understanding the choice process of the intent to study abroad. [Feature]. *Research in Higher Education, 50*(2), 119–143. doi: 10.1007/s11162-008-9111-x

Sánchez, C. M., Fornerino, M., and Zhang, M. (2006). Motivations and the intent to study abroad among U.S., French, and Chinese students. *Journal of Teaching in International Business, 18,* 27–52. doi: 10.1300/J066v18n01_03

Savicki, V. (ed.) (2008). *Developing intercultural competence and transformation: Theory, research, and application in international education.* Sterling, VA: Stylus.

Schnusenberg, O., de Jong, P., and Goel, L. (2012). Predicting study abroad intentions based on the theory of planned behavior. *Decision Sciences Journal of Innovative Education, 10*(3), 337–361. doi: 10.1111/j.1540-4609.2012.00350.x

Sell, D. K. (1983). Research on attitude change in U.S. students who participate in foreign study experiences: Past findings and suggestions for future research. *International Journal of Intercultural Relations, 7,* 131–147.

The Senator Paul Simon Study Abroad Foundation Act of 2007. HR 1469, S. 991.

Shaheen, S. (2004). *The effect of pre-departure preparation on student intercultural development during study abroad programs* (Doctoral dissertation). Ohio State University, Columbus. OH. Retrieved August 8, 2012, from search.proquest.com/pqdtft/docview/305140458 /1386CAFB16F1554FC2C/1?accountid=14556.

Siaya, L., and Hayward, F. M. (2003). *Mapping internationalization on U.S. campuses.* Washington, DC: American Council on Education.

Sommer, J. G. (2003). Globalization and the new imperative for study abroad. *Study abroad: A 21st century perspective, I.* Retrieved from www.aifsfoundation.org/21century.asp.

Souders, B. W. (2006). Now that I am home, who am I? Renegotiating American identity among returned study abroad participants. *LLC Review, 6*(1), 22–41.

Spiering, K., and Erickson, S. (2006). Study abroad as innovation: Applying the diffusion model to international education. *International Education Journal, 7,* 314–322.

Spitzberg, B. H., and Changnon, G. (2009). Conceptualizing intercultural competence. In D. K. Deardorff (Ed.), *The SAGE handbook of intercultural competence* (pp. 2–52). Thousand Oaks, CA: Sage.

Stallman, E., Woodruff, G. A., Kasravi, J., and Comp, D. (2010). The diversification of the student profile. In W. W. Hoffa and S. C. DePaul (Eds.), *A history of U.S. study abroad: 1965–present.* Lancaster, PA: Frontiers: The Interdisciplinary Journal of Study Abroad.

Stephenson, S. (2002). Beyond the lapiths and the centaurs: Cross-cultural "deepening" through study abroad. In W. Grünzweig and N. Rinehart (Eds.), *Rockin' in Red Square: Critical approaches to international education in the time of cyberculture* (pp. 85–104). Munster, Germany: Lit Verlag.

Stroud, A. H. (2010). Who plans (not) to study abroad? An examination of U.S. student intent. *Journal of Studies in International Education, 20*(10), 1–18.

Sutton, R. C., and Rubin, D. L. (2004). The GLOSSARI Project: Initial findings from a system-wide research initiative on study abroad learning outcomes. *Frontiers: The Interdisciplinary Journal of Study Abroad, 10,* 65–82.

Sutton, R. C., and Rubin, D. L. (2010). *Documenting the academic impact of study abroad.* Final report of the GLOSSARI project. Paper presented at the NAFSA Annual Conference, Kansas City, MO.

Talburt, S., and Stewart, M. A. (1999). What's the subject of study abroad? Race, gender, and "living culture." *Modern Language Journal, 83,* 163–175.

Thomas, S. L., and McMahon, M. E. (1998). Americans abroad: Student characteristics, pre-departure qualifications and performance. *International Journal of Educational Management, 12*(2), 57–64.

Toncar, M. F., Reid, J. S., and Anderson, C. E. (2005). Perceptions and preferences of study abroad: Do business students have different needs? *Journal of Teaching in International Business, 17*(1/2), 61–80. doi: 10.1300/J066v17n01_04

Tonkin, H. (Ed.). (2004). *Service-learning across cultures: Promise and achievement.* New York: International Partnership for Service Learning.

Tsantir, S. B., and Titus, B. J. (2006, Fall). Heritage-seeking and study abroad: A case study. *IIE Networker,* Fall, 27–29.

Turner, S. E., and Bowen, W. G. (1999). Choice of major: The changing (unchanging) gender gap. *Industrial and Labor Relations Review, 52*(2), 289–313.

Twombly, S. B. (1995, Fall). Piropos and friendships: Gender and culture clash in study abroad. *Frontiers: The interdisciplinary journal of study abroad, 1,* 1–27.

Twombly, S. B. (2010). PIRE Mid-Grant Evaluation. Unpublished report. University of Kansas.

University of Kansas. (n.d.) "About KU: Mission." Retrieved November, 2011, from www.ku.edu/about/mission/.

University of Minnesota. (n.d.) "SAGE (Study Abroad for Global Engagement): Beyond immediate impact." Retrieved August 9, 2012, from www.cehd.umn.edu/OLPD/SAGE/.

University of Wisconsin (n.d.). "Study abroad." Retrieved November, 2011, from www .wisconsin.edu/fadmin/fppp/fppp45.htm.

Van Der Meid, J. S. (2003). Asian Americans: Factors influencing the decision to study abroad. *Frontiers: The Interdisciplinary Journal of Study Abroad, 9,* 71–110.

Vande Berg, M. (2003). The case for assessing educational outcomes in study abroad. In G.T.M. Hult and E. C. Lashbrooke, Jr. (Eds.), *Study abroad: Perspectives and experiences from business schools* (pp. 23–36). Oxford, England: Elsevier Science.

Vande Berg, M. (2007). Intervening in the learning of U.S. students abroad. *Journal of Studies in International Education, 11*(3/4), 392–399.

Vande Berg, M. (n.d.) "Research Approach." Retrieved November, 2011, from www.forumea .org/documents/researchapproach.pdf.

Vande Berg, M., Connor-Linton, J., and Paige, M. R. (2009). The Georgetown Consortium Project: Interventions for student learning abroad. *Frontiers: The Interdisciplinary Journal of Study Abroad, 18,* 1–75.

Wallace, D. H. (1999). *Academic study abroad: The long-term impact on alumni careers, volunteer activities, world, and personal perspectives* (Doctoral dissertation). Claremont Graduate University, Claremont, CA. Retrieved August 12, 2012, from search.proquest.com/pqdtft /docview/304515457/1386CB15D0A37CB485B/6?accountid=14556.

Weaver, H. D. (1989). Research on U.S. students abroad: A bibliography with abstracts. Retrieved August 4, 2012, from globaledresearch.com/book_research_weaver.asp.

Whalen, B. (2009). Assessment and improvement: Expanding education abroad capacity and enhancing quality through standards of good practice. In P.B.R. Gutierrez (Ed.), *Expanding study abroad capacity at U.S. colleges and universities.* New York: Institute of International Education.

Wilkinson, S. (1998a). Study abroad from the participants' perspective: A challenge to common beliefs. *Foreign Language Annals, 31,* 23–49.

Wilkinson, S. (1998b). On the nature of immersion during study abroad: Some participant perspectives. *Frontiers: The Interdisciplinary Journal of Study Abroad, 4,* 121–138.

Wilkinson, S. (2000). Emerging questions about study abroad. *ADFL Bulletin, 32,* 36–41.

Williams, T. R. (2005). Exploring the impact of study abroad on students' intercultural communications skills: Adaptability and sensitivity. *Journal of Studies in International Education, 9,* 356–371.

Woolf, M. (2007). Impossible things before breakfast: Myths in education abroad. *Journal of Studies in International Education, 11*(3/4), 496–509.

Younes, M. N., and Asay, S.M. (2003). The world as a classroom: The impact of international study experiences on college students. *College Teaching*, 51(4), 141–147.

Young, D. Y. (2003). *Participation in a study-abroad program and persistence at a liberal arts university* (Doctoral dissertation). University of North Texas, Denton, TX. Retrieved August 8, 2012, from search.proquest.com/pqdtft/docview/305316624 /1386CB42 F012453EF/2?accountid=14556.

Zachrisson, C. U. (2005). New study abroad destinations: Trends and emerging opportunities. *Study abroad: A 21st century perspective, II.* Retrieved February, 2012, from www .aifsfoundation.org/21century.asp.

Zemach-Bersin, T. (2007). Global citizenship & study abroad: It's all about U.S. *Critical Literacy: Theories and Practices, 1*(2), 16–28.

Zemach-Bersin, T. (2009). Selling the world: Study abroad marketing and the privatization of global citizenship. In R. Lewin (Ed.), *The handbook of practice and research in study abroad: Higher education and the quest for global citizenship* (pp. 303–320). New York: Routledge.

Zhai, L., and Scheer, S. D. (2002). Influence of international study abroad programs on agricultural students. *Journal of International Agricultural and Extension Education, 9*(3), 23–29.

Zhang, Y. (2011). CSCC Review Series Essay: Education abroad in the U.S. community colleges. *Community College Review, 39*(2), 181–200.

Name Index

A

Adelman, C., 21
Allen, H. W., 47, 48
Allport, G. W., 71, 72
Amir, Y., 72
Anderson, A., 49, 99, 100, 101, 111
Anderson, A. A., 57
Anderson, C. E., 60
Anderson, P. H., 73
Annett, C., 54, 55, 56, 59
Armstrong, G. K., 81
Arum, S., 12
Asay, S. M., 4, 78, 79
Ashley, B., 99
Astin, A., 6
Auerbach, J., 63

B

Back, M., 81
Barrutia, R., 77
Baxter Magolda, M., 68, 71, 92
Bhandari, R., 11, 37, 38, 41, 42, 43, 62, 63
Bicknese, G., 73
Bikson, T. K., 21, 67
Biscarra, A., 7
Black, H. T., 73
Black, J. S., 92
Bloom, B., 112
Blum, D. E., 22
Bok, D., 2
Bolen, M. C., 2, 4, 20, 23, 24, 96, 97
Booker, R., 93

Bowen, W. G., 50
Bowman, J. E., 2, 15, 16, 51
Braskamp, D. C., 77
Braskamp, L. A., 77
Brecht, R., 81, 85
Brewer, E., 30, 63, 113, 114
Brint, S., 24
Brown, L. M., 44, 53, 54, 55, 57, 58
Brown, R., 71
Brux, J. M., 38, 44, 53, 54, 55, 56, 57, 58
Bu, L., 17, 18, 19, 96
Burn, B., 46, 74, 75, 80, 87, 88, 89, 91, 93, 108
Burr, P. L., 54, 55, 57
Burris, B., 22, 23, 26, 67, 94
Bush, G. W., 21

C

Calhoon, J. A., 54, 55, 56, 59
Cardon, P. W., 61
Carlson, J. S., 46, 73, 74, 75, 80, 87, 88, 89, 91, 93, 108
Changnon, G., 69
Chen, R.J.C., 48
Chickering, A., 112
Chieffo, L., 73, 75
Chmela, H., 22
Chow, P., 10
Church, A. T., 92
Churchill, E., 81, 85, 86
Citron, J. L., 4, 98, 99, 100, 101, 102, 111
Clarke, I., 4, 73, 74, 78

J

Jackson, M. J., 55
Jessup-Anger, J. E., 4
Johnston, J. S., Jr., 20
Jon, J., 90
Jones-Rikkers, C. G., 73
Jorge, E., 57
Jurgens, J. C., 77

K

Kalunian, J., 73
Kanach, N. A., 25
Kasravi, J., 19, 27, 37, 38, 40, 41, 42, 44, 50, 51, 53, 54, 55, 57, 58, 59, 62, 63, 64, 81
Kauffmann, N. L., 77
Kegan, R., 92
Kheiltash, O., 45, 46, 48, 52
Kim, D. B., 63
Kim, R. I., 46, 47, 50, 60, 93
King, L. J., 47
King, P. M., 68, 71, 92
Kitchener, K., 92
Kitsantas, A., 4, 73, 74
Knight, J., 11, 12
Koester, J., 37, 93
Kroeger, K. R., 4
Kuh, G. D., 22

L

Lambert, R. D., 37
Laubscher, M. R., 80
Law, S. A., 21
Lawton, L., 73
Levine, D. O., 16
Lewin, R., 1, 80
Lindsey, E. W., 77
Lindstrom, G., 67
Lucas, C. J., 2, 15, 16
Lucas, J. M., 40, 48, 51, 102
Luu, D. T., 22, 23, 26, 67, 94

M

McAuliffe, G., 77
McClure, K.R.S., 57
McKeown, J. S., 23, 47, 77, 79, 80, 86, 108

McKinney, J., 51
McMahon, M. E., 50, 81, 83, 86
McMillen, R. M., 4, 73, 74, 75, 78
Magnan, S. S., 81
Mahon, J., 73
Malmgren, J., 4, 84
Marshall, B., 61
Mendenhall, M., 92
Merrill, K. C., 77
Merrill, M., 6, 7, 27, 29, 34, 35
Merva, M., 82, 86
Metzger, C., 81
Meyers, J., 4, 73, 74
Mikhailova, L., 17, 18
Milstein, T., 77, 87
Mistretta, W., 81
Moini, J., 67

N

Niehaus, E., 57, 62
Norris, M. E., 81, 88, 89
Nussbaum, M., 2

O

Obst, D., 37, 38, 41, 42, 43, 62, 63
Ogden, A., 19, 97
O'Hara, S., 63
Olson, C. L., 4, 22

P

Paige, M. R., 76, 88, 91
Pascarella, E. T., 7, 38, 39, 43, 44, 45, 47, 48, 49, 50, 51, 52, 53, 54, 56, 58, 60, 62, 64, 65, 67, 73, 90, 92, 93
Patterson, P. K., 73
Paulsen, M. B., 6, 7, 38, 39, 43, 44, 45, 47, 48, 49, 50, 51, 53, 54, 56, 58, 60, 62, 64, 65, 93
Paus, E., 38, 42, 62, 64
Pearson, J., 65
Pedersen, P. J., 73
Penn, E. B., 54, 55, 56
Perdreau, C., 44, 53, 54, 55, 58
Perna, L., 38, 39
Perry, W., 92

Subject Index

Consolidated Appropriations Act (2004), 21
Costa Rican study abroad study, 100, 102
Council on International Educational
Exchange (CIEE), 7, 8, 18, 26, 33, 35,
37, 96

D

Deficit Reduction Act (2005), 21
Degree aspirations, 59–60
Discrimination fears, 58–59

E

Education abroad, 10. *See also* Study
abroad
Emory College Science Experience Abroad
(SEA), 63
Ethnic minorities. *See* Racial/ethnic
minorities
"Evolving Threads in Study Abroad
Research" (Churchill and Dufon), 85

F

Faculty-led study tours, 28
Family support, 57–58
Financial issues, 53–54, 118
"First-time effect," 79
Ford Foundation, 18, 96
Foreign exchange programs. *See* Study
abroad programs
Forum on Education Abroad, 7, 10, 19, 27,
28, 29, 31, 35, 111
*Frontiers: The Interdisciplinary Journal of
Study Abroad* (Forum on Education
Abroad), 7
Fulbright International Education
Exchange Program, 17, 18, 96

G

Gender differences: community college
student participation and, 49–50;
factors affecting men's and women's
participation, 48–52; how race and
ethnicity interact with, 49;
major/academic discipline and
participation by, 50–51; "piropoing"

(verbal harassment) experienced by
female students, 100–101; reasons for
lower male participation, 51–52; study
abroad student participation by, 41
Georgetown Consortium Project, 76, 91
Global citizenship, 98, 112
Globalization: definition of, 11; study
abroad in context of, 11–12; study
abroad outcomes for intercultural
competence and perspectives of, 68–77
GLOSSARI Project, 83, 86–87, 91
Grade point average (GPA), 81–82
Graduation rates, 82–84

H

Heritage seeking motivation, 57
*High Impact Educational Practices: What
They Are, Who Has Access to Them, and
Why They Matter* (Kuh), 22
Higher education: reframing assessment of
study abroad role in, 114–115; study
abroad outcomes for, 80–87. *See also*
Institutions; Internationalization
Higher Education Assistance Act (1965), 20
Higher Education Reconciliation Act
(2005), 21
Hispanic/Latino(a) students, 41. *See also*
Racial/ethnic minorities

I

Identity development outcome, 77–79
IES Abroad Fifty-Year Alumni Survey, 25,
88, 89
Imperialism, 96, 98
Individual human capital, 52–53
Input-Environment-Output model, 6
Institute of International Education (IIE):
Committee on the Junior Year Abroad
formed by, 16; on community college
student participation, 43; founding of
the, 16; on increased participation in
study aboard programs, 3; on number of
study abroad participants, 26; Open
Doors Report by, 18, 19, 40, 42; on
preferred destinations, 43; as primary

source of study aboard information, 7, 8; promotion of study aboard by, 96; on racial/ethnic minorities participation in study abroad, 41; role in early study abroad programs by, 16–17, 18; role in third-party provider debate by, 35; short-term programs as defined by, 28; study abroad definition by, 11, 12; as third-party provider, 33–34; "top colleges" for study abroad rankings by, 4; on types of study abroad programs, 27

Institutions: commitment to academic internationalism by, 1–4; historical context of study abroad programs of, 13–26; racial/ethnic minority study abroad barriers from, 55–56; reframing how study abroad education is assessed by, 114–115; as study abroad providers, 33. *See also* Higher education

Intellectual development, 79–80

Intercultural competence: contact hypothesis on study abroad and increased, 71–72; definition and construct of, 69–70; don't assume that studying abroad improves, 111–112; Lincoln Commission on study abroad impact on, 14, 21, 68; study abroad outcomes for, 72–77; three vectors for understanding development of, 71

International Partnership for Service Learning, 34

Internationalization: conceptual framework used to examine, 5–7; definition of, 12; increasing trend of, 1–4; purpose of outcomes of, 4–5; study abroad in context of, 11–12. *See also* Higher education; Study abroad

Iraq War, 78

J

Journal of the New England Board of Higher Education, 98

Junior Year Abroad (JYA) programs: origins and early, 15, 28; post-World War II, 17

L

Language proficiency outcome, 84–86

Latino(a) students, 41. *See also* Racial/ethnic minorities

Legislation. *See* U.S. legislation

Level-based classification system, 31–32

Liberal Learning and America's Promise (LEAP) [AAC&U], 22

Lincoln Commission. *See* Commission on the Abraham Lincoln Study Abroad Fellowship Program

M

Major/academic discipline: business students, 60–62; degree aspirations, 59–60; gender differences in participation by, 50–51; racial/ethnic minorities student participation and, 56–57; STEM students, 40, 42, 62–63, 107; study abroad outcomes for increased engagement in, 80–87; as study abroad participation factor, 42

Making the World Like Us (Bu), 98

Measure of Intellectual Development (MID), 79

Minority students. *See* Racial/ethnic minorities

Motivations: heritage seeking, 57; as study abroad factor, 47–48

Mount Holyoke, 1–2

Multiple-criterion classification schemes, 30–32

Multiracial students, 41. *See also* Racial/ethnic minorities

N

NAFSA, 3, 14, 18, 21, 27, 35, 40, 69, 93

National Center for Education Statistics (NCES), 23

National Commission on Terrorist Attacks Upon the United States (the 9/11 Commission), 21

National Defense Education Act (1957), 17

National Science Foundation (NSF), 62

National Sciences and Mathematics Access to Retain Talent (SMART) Grants, 21
National Survey of Student Engagement, 24
National Task Force on Undergraduate Education Abroad, 14, 69
Native American/Alaskan Native students, 41
9/11 attacks, 20, 23
9/11 Commission, 21
No Child Left Behind (NCLB), 117

O

Open Doors Report (IIE), 40, 42
The "other," 78
Outcomes. *See* Study abroad outcomes
"An Overview of Issues and Research in Language Learning in a Study Abroad Setting" (Freed), 85

P

Peace Corps, 17
"Piropoing" (verbal harassment), 100–101
Post-Vietnam War era, 19–20
Post-World War II era, 17–19
Preferred destinations, 43
Providers: common organizational frameworks for, 33; third-party, 33–35
PRWeb, 25

R

Racial/ethnic minorities: family support as participation factor, 57–58; fears of discrimination by, 58–59; financial factor affecting participation by, 53–54, 118; heritage seeking participation motivation by, 57; how gender differences in participation interact with, 49; individual and human capital factor affecting participation by, 52–53; institutional barriers to participation by, 55–56; lack of role models affecting participation by, 55; major and program fit factor and participation by, 56–57; perceptions of who should study abroad affecting participation by, 54–55; study abroad student participation by, 41. *See also specific population*
"Reverse culture shock," 75
Rockin' in Red Square: Critical Approaches to International Education in the Age of Cyberspace (Grünzweig and Rinehart), 98
Role models, 55

S

SAEP (Study Abroad Evaluation Project), 46–47, 75–76, 88, 91
SAGE (Study Abroad for Global Engagement) project, 88, 90
The Senator Paul Simon Study Aboard Foundation Act (2007), 3, 21, 22
Smith-Mundt Act (1948), 17
Socioeconomic status, 44
Standards of Good Practices for Education Abroad, 111
STEM students: disciplinary and institutional barriers to participation by, 107; examining the reasons for less participation by, 40, 62–63; increasing study abroad participation by, 42, 107
Strategic Task Force on Education Abroad (NAFSA), 21
Students: attitudes toward study abroad by, 46–47; community college, 43, 49–50, 63–64; demographics of those who study abroad, 37–38, 39–43; factors affecting intent to study abroad by, 44–63; individual motivations for study abroad by, 47–48; percentage who study abroad, 37; predisposition to study abroad by, 45; study abroad participation by community college, 63–64
Study abroad: conceptual framework used to examine, 5–7; critical studies of the study abroad experience, 100–103; critiques of unstated purposes of study

University System of Georgia, 92
University of Wisconsin, 10
U.S. Agency for International
    Development, 17, 18
U.S. Department of Education, 90
U.S. imperialism, 96, 98
U.S. legislation: Deficit Reduction Act
    (2005), 21; Higher Education Assistance
    Act (1965), 20; Higher Education
    Reconciliation Act (2005), 21; National
    Defense Education Act (1957), 17; No
    Child Left Behind (NCLB), 117; The
    Senator Paul Simon Study Aboard

Foundation Act (2007), 3, 21, 22;
    Smith-Mundt Act (1948), 17
U.S. State Department, 17, 18
UT-Austin study, 83

W

Wabash National Study of Liberal Arts
    Education, 9, 39, 76
Wesleyan University, 102
World Bank, 18

Y

"The Year of Study Abroad" (2006), 21

About the Authors

Susan B. Twombly is professor of higher education and chair of the Department of Educational Leadership and Policy Studies at the University of Kansas. She is past vice president of AERA Division J. She served as a Fulbright Fellow in Ecuador in 1995. Her research focuses on women in higher education, faculty, and community colleges. Most recently she and her colleagues have been working on a series of studies of international faculty in U.S. colleges and universities. She serves on the board of Latin American Studies at the University of Kansas.

Mark H. Salisbury is assistant dean and director of institutional research and assessment at Augustana College in Rock Island, Illinois. He is also a researcher with the Wabash National Study on Liberal Arts Education and a Teagle Assessment Scholar. His research examines both the factors that might predict participation in and the educational outcomes of study abroad. He was a co-principal investigator for the University of Iowa's Internationalization Assessment Project as a part of the American Council on Education's Internationalization Laboratory. Mark earned his PhD in higher education from the University of Iowa.

Shannon D. Tumanut is an adjunct associate professor of English for academic purposes at Johnson County Community College in Overland Park, Kansas, and a PhD student in educational leadership and policy studies at the University of Kansas. Her current research interests focus on language and identity as they relate to second/foreign language pedagogy in higher education, particularly at the community college level.

Paul Klute is assistant to the senior vice provost for academic affairs and principal analyst in the Office of Institutional Research and Planning at the University of Kansas. He is also a PhD student in educational leadership and policy studies at the University of Kansas. His current research interests focus on assessment practices and strategic planning in higher education.

About the ASHE Higher Education Report Series

Since 1983, the ASHE (formerly ASHE-ERIC) Higher Education Report Series has been providing researchers, scholars, and practitioners with timely and substantive information on the critical issues facing higher education. Each monograph presents a definitive analysis of a higher education problem or issue, based on a thorough synthesis of significant literature and institutional experiences. Topics range from planning to diversity and multiculturalism, to performance indicators, to curricular innovations. The mission of the Series is to link the best of higher education research and practice to inform decision making and policy. The reports connect conventional wisdom with research and are designed to help busy individuals keep up with the higher education literature. Authors are scholars and practitioners in the academic community. Each report includes an executive summary, review of the pertinent literature, descriptions of effective educational practices, and a summary of key issues to keep in mind to improve educational policies and practice.

The Series is one of the most peer reviewed in higher education. A National Advisory Board made up of ASHE members reviews proposals. A National Review Board of ASHE scholars and practitioners reviews completed manuscripts. Six monographs are published each year and they are approximately 144 pages in length. The reports are widely disseminated through Jossey-Bass and John Wiley & Sons, and they are available online to subscribing institutions through Wiley Online Library (http://wileyonlinelibrary.com).

Call for Proposals

The ASHE Higher Education Report Series is actively looking for proposals. We encourage you to contact one of the editors, Dr. Kelly Ward (kaward@wsu.edu) or Dr. Lisa Wolf-Wendel (lwolf@ku.edu), with your ideas.

Recent Titles

CPSIA information can be obtained at www.ICGtesting.com
Printed in the USA
BVOW03s2024041013
332855BV00005B/5/P